Vietnam Memories:
A Cookbook

by
Bich Nga Burrill

www.trafford.com

North America & international
toll-free: 1 888 232 4444 (USA & Canada)
fax: 812 355 4082

Acknowledgements:

THANK YOU, VIETNAM, FOR THE MEMORIES.

Thank you to my family for their love and support.

Special thanks to Kay Retzlaff for helping me with this book, for making me laugh and being my number one fan.

Thank you Matt Gerald for all the gorgeous flower props.

Thank you Robin Farin for the beautiful photographs featured in my book.

Thank you to all my friends/customers who show up every weekend at the Farmers' markets from Bangor to Bar Harbor, Maine, regardless of the weather. You're the people who have inspired me week after week. Because of you, I'll never stop challenging myself in the kitchen.

And, last but not least, thank you, Dear Reader, for taking time out to travel with me. Better yet, if you cook along as you read, then all the hard work of writing the book has already paid off. I can't really say it's been all work, for the writing has been a healing process for me. Soon, I hope to go back to Vietnam. This time, I will be there with a different attitude. I hope to travel from the North to the South to see how much the culinary life and the people have changed in 30 years. Maybe then I can write a new chapter, or, perhaps, even another, memory cookbook.

From my love of cooking and the passion for good food, I hope to have inspired you.

Table of Contents

Vietnam

VIETNAM WAS RULED BY THE CHINESE FOR A THOUSAND YEARS. THEN the French came and stayed for almost a century. It is surrounded by China to the north, Laos and Cambodia to the west and the Philippines and Thailand to the east, Malaysia and Indonesia to the southeast. Vietnam is shaped like the letter "s". It's about three quarters the size of California, with the Red River Delta in the north and the Mekong Delta in the South. There are only two seasons in Vietnam—the wet season in summer and the dry season in winter. Some have called Vietnam the "Gem of the Orient," the "Paris of the Orient," and "The Crossroads of the Asian World." Whatever other people have called it, I called it home for 24 years.

The Vietnamese food culture has been influenced by the Chinese, as evidenced by stir fry, deep fry, noodles, tofu, and, of course, soy sauce. Our famous Beef with Rice Noodles from Northern Vietnam was started by the Mongolian invasion in the thirteenth century. The French left an imprint as well. French bread, pastries and luxuries, such as butter and cream, have influenced Vietnamese cuisine. Vietnam has taken these influences and from them created its own unique food culture.

The regions of Vietnam have contributed to that culture. Northern Vietnam, which is where I was born, has a milder cuisine. Not many spices were available. The climate in the north is cold, so soup, stew and congee (rice soup) are popular. There is also some stir fry. We also like tidbits of food dipped into hot broth or sliced marinated meat grilled over charcoal fires.

The center of Vietnam is an area called "Royal Palace," which offers a spicier cuisine. It is famous for rice noodle soup with pork and beef. The broth is heavily spiced with shrimp paste, chilies and lemongrass. This soup became a national treasure. Another specialty is *nem*, a dollop of fermented pork laced with garlic and birds eye chilies, wrapped tightly in banana leaves.

The spiciest food of all the regions is that of the South, (where my family moved in 1954), which has more stir fry and quick cooking techniques. The fast cooking means cooks aren't slaving over hot stoves in a steaming climate for hours. There was no refrigeration when I was growing up, so food was bought, cooked and eaten all in the same day. This meant that everything was fresh. The warm weather also affects the way food is eaten. Varieties of barbecue meats are always served with cool, fresh vegetables and herbs. One well known dish is grilled beef with lemongrass and chilies wrapped in moist rice paper. This is served with lettuce, cucumber, mint, cilantro, basil and dipped into a spicy and hot *nuoc cham* to deliver a symphony of taste.

There are variations on this way of eating. A favorite dish is *cha tom*, shrimp paste, wrapped around sugar cane, then grilled over charcoal. The best part of the food is the fresh and exotic fruits, such as *logan, ramputant, durian,* many kinds of bananas and mangoes, which are available throughout the year. All provide the cooling elements for a tropical climate.

Eating wasn't just about "filling a hole." We celebrated everything with food.

Learning to Cook

THE FIRST COOKING LESSON FROM MY MOTHER WAS HOW TO prepare Steamed Duck with Eight Treasures. I was barely 10 years old. Some forty-odd years later I'm still cooking and, of course, still learning. As long as I can remember on happy occasions and special events, food was always the center of activities.

Because I was the oldest female child, before I was even a teenager, one of my chores was to plan the meals for the whole family. Early in the morning my mother would hand me some money and a basket. I would happily skip all the way to the market where I would dicker my way to the best food at the best price. My goal was to have some money left over so that I could buy myself a special treat to eat on the way home.

There's no doubt that I learned my cooking skills from my mother. She's a very good and clever cook, and it shows through, from every-day meals to special occasions. She never used or owned a cookbook, nor did she have a fancy, equipped kitchen. The gadget she used the most was a pair of regular chopsticks. When you don't have much to work with, your eyes are measuring cups and your hands provide the power.

My mother, who was from the North, taught me a lot about Northern Vietnamese cuisine. Because of the size of the family, (I was the eldest of eight), and the fact that both parents worked, we had domestic help at home. But, my mother always did the cooking.

As a young teen, I was able to select a live chicken, dress it, and turn it into three different dishes. I cooked with duck, frog and all kinds of fish. I was able to identify herbs and spices by both sight and smell. I didn't realize it then, but I had started on the road to becoming the gourmet cook I am today. As I grew older and began working away from home, one of my goals was to eat in as many different restaurants as possible and to compare dishes and tastes.

This was fun, and, at the same time, I got to learn more about the foods from region to region. Each restaurant or food vendor had its own special kind of dish, and these cooks jealously guarded their cooking secrets. In Vietnam you are not obligated to list or give out information about ingredients. Most people didn't care to ask, but I did. I always had questions. Sometimes I would get an answer, but in most cases I was able to figure out what the ingredients were by taste and smell. This became a trait I still use today.

Chapter One

SAIGON CHILDHOOD

Saigon

ONCE UPON A TIME, SAIGON WAS A VERY POPULAR PLACE. I HAVE ALWAYS considered the city to have a personality, like a close girlfriend. Saigon has always been "she" in my vocabulary. For a good part of my life, she was the place where I went when I wanted to get away from it all. Saigon would come to my rescue when things were so wrong, and if I wanted to have fun, Saigon was it. From cafés beside Le Loi Boulevard, to flower shops, to ice cream parlors, to movie theaters, to night clubs, to wonderful restaurants, Saigon had it all. It never mattered what kind of mood I was in, when I was in Saigon, I was in heaven.

She's still there, across the ocean, but my heaven no longer exists. I'll go back some day, but I'll be visiting another place with a different name. I guess I shall have to learn how to let go of the old Saigon some day. I don't know how or when, because, after all these years, the wound is still there.

Saigon Hot Chicken

THIS IS TRULY THE ESSENCE OF VIETNAMESE CUISINE, SPICY AND hot, sweet and salty. It's all about chemistry at its best.

> 1 fryer chicken, trimmed of fat, cut into bite size pieces or 3-4 lbs. boneless chicken breasts

Spice:
  3 stalks of lemongrass (remove the tough part)
  ¼ c. garlic
  2-10 birds eye chilies or Thai Dragon
  1 T. garlic oil
  1 T. shallot oil or 2 T. vegetable oil
  1 T. sugar
  ½ tsp. salt

In food processor, turn spice into paste. Mix paste with cut up chicken pieces. This step can be done a day ahead.

Sauce:
  ¼ c. fish sauce (there is no substitute here)
  1 T. dark soy sauce
  ½ c. broth or water

Have ¼ c. brown sugar ready

In a hot wok with high heat, drizzled with 2 or 3 T. oil, sear the chicken pieces. Do it in 3 or 4 batches. This is an important step. Remove each batch. Let wok heat up again before you add more chicken. If it burns a little bit, that's good. When the last batch is removed from wok, sprinkle in the brown sugar and let it caramelize. Don't worry about the smoke. Just don't burn the sugar. Return the chicken to the wok for the next 3 to 4 minutes. Keep stirring. Then add sauce. Stir well. Cover. Cook for 7-10 minutes. Open up. The cooking process is done when the sauce clings to meat, but isn't runny.

Garnish with scallion and cilantro (1/2 c. mixed)

Tip: When a recipe calls for searing, use the highest heat possible. Never crowd the pan.

Auntie Quang and Her Lard

AUNTIE QUANG LIVED JUST A FEW HOUSES DOWN THE ROAD. I HUNG OUT at her house a lot—for a good reason. I liked her son. He was so-o-o cute. I couldn't help wondering why. Auntie Quang was a large framed woman, wide and tall. His father looked like a shrimp next to her. The pair of them looked like an illustration for "Jack Sprat," not to be mean or cruel. I had such a crush on that guy. I think he knew that, but he treated me like the sister he had never had.

When you hang out at someone's house a lot, you peek into their eating habits. I noticed Auntie Quang would always buy water spinach by the bushel day after day, week after week. I couldn't help myself. "Auntie Quang, I see you buy a lot of water spinach. You must know a lot of ways to prepare it. Why don't you share some of your dishes with me?"

Very seriously, she gushed, "No, I just cook them with a lot of lard. You just can't go wrong with lard, even if all you have is grass. I bet you lard would make that taste delicious as well. Lucky for me, water spinach is cheap and plentiful."

I guess she answered my culinary curiosity. Good thing I didn't take Auntie Quang's advice for my water spinach repertoire.

Nanny's Pork Chop

THE HEAVENLY SCENT OF GARLIC IN PORK CHOP, LACED WITH IRRESISTIBLE sweet and salty shallot sauce, nested on top of a pile of tender crisp green beans, is the aroma of my favorite childhood comfort food. Give this to me, with a bowl of rice and some *nu'o'c cham* and I'll die happy. This is still one of my favorite meals, even though I have become a much more sophisticated cook over the years.

I learned the recipe from my nanny. She cooked, took care of us and loved us until she passed away. She was a tiny little lady with a determined voice. I never knew my grandparents, so I gave all my love to nanny. To us kids, she was never a hired helper. She was one of us.

We never got more than one pork chop at any meal—except for my sister. She inhaled her pork chop, then moved her greedy little paws toward nanny's. I winked at nanny and remarked, "The pork chop is kind of salty," hoping to slow down my sister's eating process. All I wanted to do was save my nanny from losing it all, but, of course, my sister didn't care. She ignored me and went on smacking her little lips, saying, "Yes, it's salty, but in a very delicious way."

I gave up. Over the years, I just watched my little sister playing "the pork chop invader" game with nanny.

Nanny's Pork Chop

4 pork chops

Mix and rub over meat:
2 T. finely pasted garlic
¼ t. salt
¼ t. pepper
2-3 large cloved shallots, thinly sliced
1-2 T. brown sugar

Mix:
¾ c. broth or water
2 T. fish or soy sauce

2 stalks scallion, cut into ½ inch pieces
2 lbs. fresh string beans, trimmed and washed

Before starting to cook the meat, put beans into a steamer and start to steam.

Heat a large, heavy skillet on high heat until very hot. Swirl in 1-2 T. canola oil. When oil begins to smoke, sear pork on both sides. Depending on how hot your stove is, this step will take three to five minutes. Remove meat. Clean up all residues.

Replace the pan on the heat. Add 1 T. oil. Let the oil heat until very hot, then add shallot. Stir constantly for two minutes. Add sugar. At this point, watch it like a hawk and keep stirring. When the color changes from light brown to mahogany, immediately add water and sauce. Mix well, then return meat to the pan. Swirl the meat around the sauce. Cover. Cook seven to 10 minutes. Turn the meat once at about the mid point. Add scallion.

The vegetables should be cooked. Put beans on a large deep plate. Arrange meat beautifully on top. Scrape and drizzle sauce over the meat and serve with rice, of course.

What you should have is a beautiful dish to feast your eyes, as well as a delicious meal to please your taste buds.

By the way, I have this dish with mashed potatoes sometimes, and it's not bad. I wonder if nanny would approve. She never had mashed potatoes. I would love to be able to cook just one meal for my old nanny and to say thank you for all the meals she served us.

The Power of Chocolate

I LOVE FOOD, PERHAPS A LITTLE MORE THAN THE NEXT PERSON WHO comes along. But, I really cannot blame myself any more than I can claim that it is my own unique quality. Just ask any Vietnamese person you know. They'll tell you—there is a little obsession with food in everyone of us. The lady I met at a family gathering, once upon a time, will testify to that.

She was seated there and watched over the buffet table like a hawk. I don't think she was very happy when three or four of us teenagers piled food onto our plates. She couldn't help herself. With a Roseanne Barr kind of voice, she started preaching: "Now, now. Let's not forget that we eat to live, blah, blah, blah..."

It seemed to work, because all the kids stopped dishing food onto their plates, except me. I wasn't about to let her advice interfere with my good deal. With the sweetest, kindest voice I could muster, I told the dear old lady that she could do it her way, I was happy with mine.

Actually, my first vivid memory I have of food was when I was very very young, only three or four, before we moved to the South of Vietnam in 1954. One day, playing outside with the neighborhood kids, I noticed that suddenly there was a shadow over us. I looked up. The man before us was a towering giant, and he didn't resemble anyone I had ever known before. He was talking to us, but I didn't know what he was saying. I didn't understand his language. Before he left, he gave each of us something from his pocket, which he motioned us to eat.

When I unwrapped it and put it in my mouth, I found it was sweet. It was creamy and it was powerful. For years, I thought this was just a dream until my mother told me that this had been my first encounter with chocolate, given to me and the other children by a French man who had visited our village. Until this day, it's okay if anyone calls me a chocolate snob, because I don't waste my calories on any chocolate other than the best. I blame the French man.

Moon Cake Parade

I NEVER LOVED SCHOOL, BUT THE GRADE SCHOOL PARADE ONE YEAR stayed fresh in my memory.

They called it "The Moon Celebration Parade." We got to dress up. The starting line was at the school. Each of us held a colorful paper lantern. We marched to live music. We would go through town and back to the school. Then, we would all get a treat. In Vietnamese, this festival is called *Tet Trung Thu*, the mid-autumn festival.

I really didn't care much for dress up, and I cared even less about the marching. I was there for the moon cake. This treat was a flakey pastry wrapped around sweet lotus or black bean paste. It has remained my favorite treat to this day.

That particular year, my partner was a boy. I think he had a crush on me. I kept catching him looking at me in class quite often.

We had to hold hands with our partners. I told him the only way I would let him hold my hand was if he would sacrifice his treat to me. Otherwise, it was no deal.

Well, I had two cakes that year, along with the excitement of discovering the power I had over members of the opposite sex.

At home, once a year, my mother would make moon cake for us. She made it with lotus seed or with beans and salted egg yolks. Her recipe called for lard in the pastry, but if that's an issue, you may use shortening, but I have to confess that I prefer lard. Shortening changes the smell of moon cake, and it can't take me back to my childhood as quickly—or as heavenly—as can moon cake made with lard. I guess some things just can't be substituted.

Moon Cake

Fillings:
  1 lb black beans, sorted, rinsed and soaked over night, drained
  1 ¾ c. sugar
  ¼ c. lard or vegetable oil
  ¼ t. salt
  1 t. vanilla

Pastry—There are two doughs here:
  Dough #1—
  2 c. pastry flour
  5 T. lard
  7-8 T. cold water
  ¼ t. salt

Cut lard into the flour and salt until in pea-sized lumps. Add the water and knead until the dough is elastic. Set aside.

Dough #2*
  1 c. pastry flour
  5 T. lard
  ¼ t. salt
  *Note: There is no water in Dough #2. Cut the lard into the flour and salt mixture. Knead until the dough is soft and pliable. The dough is very easy to work with.

Roll Dough #1 into a rectangle, roughly 12 x 8 inches. Set aside. Roll Dough #2 to a slightly smaller rectangle than Dough #1. Put Dough #2 on top of Dough #1. With the long side, roll into a log. At this point, the dough may be wrapped in waxed paper and refrigerated until needed.

While the dough is in the refrigerator, make the filling. Put the beans that you've soaked overnight and drained into a large pot with 8 cups of fresh water with 1 teaspoon of baking soda. (The baking soda will reduce cooking time and will make the beans more tender.) Bring to a boil, then reduce to a simmer for 30 minutes. Drain. Put the beans in a food processor and puree into a thick paste.

In a large and deep nonstick skillet, add sugar and let it melt a little. Add beans. Stir until the sugar and beans are fully blended. Add lard or vegetable oil. Keep stirring over a low heat for 10 to 15 minutes until it forms a smooth paste. Cool until you can work it with your hands comfortably. Make 20 balls (about the size of walnuts). Flatten the balls with the palm of your hand.

Pull the pastry log from the refrigerator and cut into 20 medallions. Roll each piece into a 3 inch circle. Place the flattened bean medallion on top of the dough circle, gather the edges of the dough around the bean filling and pinch to seal. Put seal side down on a cookie sheet. Brush the pastries with an egg wash if desired.** The egg wash makes the pastry look pretty. Bake at 350 degrees for 20 minutes.

Moon cakes without egg wash will remain fresh at room temperature for a week if kept in an air tight container. They also freeze well.

**Egg wash is made with 1 egg yolk blended thoroughly with 2 T. of cold water and brushed on with a pastry brush.

Eggroll with Shiitake Mushroom and Leeks

She was always there, sitting quietly in the corner of the open market. She had a bamboo basket full of golden, crispy vegetable egg rolls. For the longest time, I always tried to finagle the household expense money so I could buy myself a treat at the market. I always bought one of her rolls and savored it all the way home. She was my model. This was the way an egg roll was supposed to taste.

Then one day, the corner was empty. This went on for weeks. Out of curiosity, I asked around. She had lost her husband, then her only son, in the same damn war. Then, she lost her will to live, and she ended her life with a chair and a rope. The war claimed another victim.

This recipe is her legacy.

Eggroll with Shiitake Mushroom and Leeks
- 3 T. hoisin sauce
- 1 t. chili garlic paste
- 8 oz. leeks, white part only, shredded
- 8 oz. fresh shiitake mushroom, sliced thin
- 1 lb shredded cabbage (napa is best)
- 2 oz. bean thread, soaked in warm water, cut into 2 inch segments
- 1 t. salt
- 1 t. black pepper
- 2 T. oyster sauce
- 1 package egg roll wrappers

In hot wok with 2 T. soybean or canola oil, sauté the hoisin and chili garlic paste for 1-2 minutes, then add the leeks. When the leeks are aromatic, (approximately 2-3 minutes), add mushrooms and cabbage, bean thread, salt, pepper, oyster sauce.

Transfer everything to a colander and let the mixture drain (probably an hour). Then refrigerate.

You can roll everything the following day.

Paste to seal the egg roll wrapper:
  1 T. flour
  2 T. water

Make sure you roll the wrappers tightly. Fry in 350 degree oil until golden (from 3-5 minutes). Turn frequently. Fry 5-6 at one time—no more. Drain on paper towel. Don't store in an air-tight container, because it will make them limp. Best served right away. This recipe will make 20 rolls.

Special Treats

Years later, when I worked at Bien Hoa Air Base during the height of the Vietnam War, when I wished I was a small child again, safe in my parents' house, before I learned about war and casualties. My childhood had been full of sweet memories—sugary sweet, that is!

Every mid-morning from 9-11, every mid afternoon from 2-4, was when the sweet vendor strolled by. And if that weren't bad enough, from 6 to 11 p.m. on every street corner in the neighborhood, the Chinese Vietnamese would be selling sweet seductions from their stalls.

I had two favorite places. One sold all kinds of fried dough. The other had at least a dozen different kinds of hot and cold sweet soups, puddings, etc.

Sesame Puff

WHENEVER I COULD, I WOULD VISIT MY FAVORITE FRIED DOUGH STALL and purchase one of these heavenly sesame puffs, which aren't as sweet as American doughnuts. The trick to making the dough puff is to keep the dough moving with a metal spatula after you place it in the hot oil. Keep turning the dough around until it's puffed up four or five times its original size.

The result is a golden, lightly sweet and nutty bread that my daughter Samantha loves (as does most any one I have ever served it to).

The oil temperature is important. Low temperature will make the dough absorb more oil. We don't want that to happen any more than we want it to turn golden before it's cooked through. Modern technology has given us the bread machine. Use it. It makes the task painless.

Mix well and knead until soft elastic.
    1 c. warm water
    1 package yeast
    1/3 c. sugar
    ½ tsp. salt
    1 tsp. baking powder
    3 c. flour

Garnish:
    ¼ c. sesame for dipping the dough into

Let the dough rest one hour. Punch down. Divide the dough into 12 balls. Dip one side into sesame seeds. Let the dough rest 10 minutes. On a lightly floured surface, roll the ball with a rolling pin until it is ¼ inch thick. The circumference should be the size of your palm.

Heat oil to 350 degrees. Fry as described above. The time needed will depend on how fast and sure your hand is. The whole cooking process should take only about five minutes total for all 12 puffs.

Autumn in Paris, page 41

Spring Rolls with Pork and Shrimp

Spring Rolls with Pork and Shrimp

On special occasions, my mother would make spring rolls. It's a painstaking process, picking the meat out of mud crabs, blending it with hand chopped pork, then mixing the meat mixture with jicama, carrots delicately seasoned with shallot and garlic. This is one of the many things that made my childhood a heaven.

    1 lb. ground pork
    8 oz. shrimp, chopped
    8 oz. jicama, thin julienne cut, water squeezed out*
    4 oz. shredded carrots, water squeezed out*
    2 t. sugar
    1 t. salt
    1 t. black pepper
    1 T. oyster sauce
    ¼ c. finely chopped onions or shallots
    1 egg
    1 package of 25 frozen spring roll pastry, thawed

Mix all ingredients together. Use an ice cream scoop to measure out the stuffing. Drop mixture in the corner of the pastry. Roll up tightly. Seal with paste.

Paste:
    2 T. flour
    ¼ c. water

Fry at 350 degrees until golden. Don't crowd the pan. Cook only 5-6 at a time for 5-6 minutes. (This egg roll has meat, so it has to be cooked a little longer.) Drain on paper towels. Don't store in an air-tight container. This will make 25 rolls.

*To squeeze out water, divide the vegetables into 2-3 batches. Use cheesecloth.

To serve this dish in traditional Vietnamese style, serve with a platter of vegetables, such as Bibb lettuce, bean sprouts, and herbs such as cilantro and mint, and dipping sauce. Cut each spring roll into thirds. Put the spring roll between lettuce and herb and dip into salad dressing fish sauce.

Uncle Ha's Cinnamon Treat

Bac Ha lived next door to us. We called him uncle, but he wasn't really related to us in any way. I was about nine or ten, and I had my own reason for hanging around his house.

Bac Ha ran a very successful business making steamed pork rolls and cinnamon pork. It was hard work and took a lot of sheer physical strength. All you had to do was watch him and his crew at work. Each man faced a huge stone mortar with a set of custom made heavy wooden pestles. They would get into a rhythm—up with the right hand, down with the left. They pounded pieces of pork into silky pink ribbons. At that point the seasoning was added. Then the process continued. They would wrap a dollop of the mixture into banana leaves. Then these individually wrapped pieces of pork were boiled for hours. This roll was called *cha lua*.

Some of the pounded pork mixture was mixed with cinnamon. This was then pasted around a hollow steel mold, which was then slowly grilled over a fire, (like a rotisserie). The finished product was called *cha que*. The ingredients may sound simple, and they are, but your mouth will tell you that you have bitten into something special. The magic is in the crunch and the sweetness of the meat, singing all the way into your stomach. The secret ingredient was the pounding of the meat into pulp.

Bac Ha taught me a very important business lesson. All I need is to be really good at one thing, then I'll be okay. Until this day, nobody, including me, can make better *cha lua* and *cha que*—even with all the fancy equipment. He really spoiled it for me.

We moved away from him, and my heart was broken. It wasn't because I missed watching Bac Ha and his crew with their gorgeous bodies at work. I was just a kid, what did I care about that? Who do you think had the honor of consuming most of the trimmings from the cinnamon pork everyday?

If you go beyond the basic tastes of sweet, sour, salty and bitter, there is a fifth flavor. In Japanese, this term is *umami*, which can be described as meaty, earthy, robust and savory. *Umami* rich foods are red meat, white meat, mushrooms, mussels, shrimp, etc.

On the other hand, you have food that has no taste at all, such as tofu, jicama, cabbage, etc. So what can the cook do to make the bland food taste good? You combine bland with *umami* rich foods, then enhance it with sauces that deliver *umami*, such as fish sauce, soy sauce, Golden Mountain Thai soy sauce, Maggie Swiss soy sauce. Now you've learned one of my secrets.

You'll need a food processor to make cinnamon pork.

Umami Dearest Pork

1 lb. pork loin, cut into small cubes (weigh after all the unwanted gristle and fat has been trimmed away)
8 oz. chicken breast, cut into small cubes
3 T. chicken broth
3 T. fish sauce
1 t. baking powder
1 t. sugar
1 t. coarse ground black pepper
1 T. potato starch
2 t. sesame oil
1 t. cinnamon, preferably Saigon cinnamon

Combine all the ingredients in a bowl. Toss well and let sit to marinate at least two hours or overnight. Before processing, place the meat in the freezer for 20 to 30 minutes. It is easier to handle when it's a little cold. Place mixture in the food processor and process it until it turns pinkish paste. Scrape the sides of the processor bowl occasionally. The product is ready to cook when it turns pink and springs back to the touch.

Divide paste into six disks. Grease your palms with vegetable oil and flatten the meat disks until they are about ½ inch thick. Lay meat patties on a heated grill. Cook the meat thoroughly. Turn once.

To pan fry: In large skillet with enough oil to coat the bottom of the pan, heat the oil on medium high. Cook the meat until golden brown on both sides.

To steam: Wrap paste in a piece of banana leaf. Steam on high heat for 20 to 30 minutes.

Serve the meat cold or at room temperature, over noodles, or over soup, or over salad, or just the way it is. It is a no guilt snack!

Temple Salad

THERE WAS NEVER ANY EASY TIME BETWEEN THE GOVERNMENT AND THE Buddhist religion. A lot of people often got thrown into the middle of the mess. At one point, students got pulled out of school to participate in Temple protests. To be honest, not all of us knew what we were fighting for.

I never was a model student. I always daydreamed in class, and I couldn't pay enough attention to any teacher, so when there was a chance to get out of school, I would jump at it. I especially loved going to the Temple, because sometimes they fed us.

One day, there was a big event. A lot of schools were involved. We got dropped right outside the Temple gate. I noticed him, out of the hundreds of people there. He was the leader. He made a speech from the top bleacher. His voice was filled with compassion. His eyes welled with tears. I was captivated. He knew what he was fighting for, and he was passionate about it. I just happened to be there. For the rest of the day, I followed him around like a puppy. At the lunch table, I managed to grab the seat across from him, and I think he noticed me.

We never spoke a word to each other, but every time our eyes met, my heart raced. He passed me the pepper. Our fingers touched, and I felt electricity.

My heart ached at the end of that day when my hero disappeared with his own crowd, and I had to return with mine. We never ran into each other again.

Does he ever think of the salad we shared that day? I wonder.

Temple Salad

Any vegetables can be used raw in this salad, with the exception of pea pods. You'll need to blanch these in boiling water before use. Carrots, cabbages, green broccoli stems, daikon, celery, bell peppers are all fine. You'll need approximately 6-7 cups of any mix and match of the above ingredients. Julienne cut everything. Sprinkle with 1 T. salt. Let set for 2 hours or overnight.

Rinse and squeeze out all moisture. This step is very important.

Mix:
2 oz. bean thread, soaked for ½ hour, blanched in boiling water
6 cups of the prepared vegetables, as directed above
1 egg crepe (see the recipe elsewhere in this book)
2 T. toasted sesame seeds
½ c. mixture of cilantro and mint

Dressing:
2 T. rice vinegar
2 T. mirin sweet wine
1 T. sesame oil
2 tsp. hot oil (optional)
3 T. sugar
2-3 T. light soy sauce
½ tsp. black pepper
3 large cloves of garlic, finely chopped
1 T. grated fresh ginger

Whisk dressing together. Pour over vegetables and bean thread. Mix well with egg crepe and toasted sesame. Garnish with herbs (cilantro and mint). Best served the same day as made. Serves 6-8.

Pickled Hot Peppers

THIS IS MY SECRET WEAPON FOR SALADS. THE HOT PEPPERS CAN BE EATEN right out of the jar, or crushed, then added to salad dressing. (See the recipe that follows.)

The pickle juice intensifies any tomato sauce. You can buy this item at the grocery store, but, of course, it doesn't taste as good.

Making pickled hot peppers is one of my prized annual projects. It marks the end of every summer.

For every quart jar and depending on the size (or kind) of pepper you use, you'll need:

> 1 lb. – 1 ¼ lb. peppers
> 8-10 cloves garlic

> **Brine:**
> 1 c. water
> 1 ½ c. white vinegar
> 1 T. pickling salt
> 1 T. sugar

I usually mix the varieties of peppers, depending on what is ready in the garden. If you can't stand the heat, make it with different colors of bell peppers instead.* This is a basic brine. You will need to experiment with different herbs to give it your own distinctive taste.

Bring the brine to a boil, pack the pepper, alternating with garlic, in a quart jar. Pour in the hot brine. Seal the jar. Put in a hot water bath for 10 minutes.

Use the brine in salad dressing.

*Here are some of my favorite pepper mixes: Hungarian wax peppers with Thai Dragon, or Jalapeno with hot cherry peppers. Makes 1 quart or 2 pints.

Cole Slaw

In a large bowl:
   7 c. sliced cabbage
   1 c. small julienne cut carrot
   1 T. salt

Mix well. Let it rest for one hour. Squeeze out all the moisture.

Dressing:
   3 T. sugar
   1 tsp. salt
   2 T. white or champagne vinegar
   1 T. hot pickle pepper vinegar
   2 T. minced hot pepper pickle
   1 large shallot bulb, finely chopped
   ½ tsp. black pepper
   3 T. shallot oil

Whisk dressing until well blended. Pour over vegetables. Mix with your hands.
Serve chilled. Garnish with crispy shallots, if desired.

Pickled Mustard Greens

EVEN IF YOU CAN EASILY FIND PICKLED MUSTARD GREENS AT specialty Asian food stores, you will find those that you make at home are much better.

For every 3-4 pounds of mustard greens, you'll need:
6 c. water
4 T. salt
4 T. sugar

Bring this mixture to a boil.

Wash the greens, trim and shake off excess water. Pack tightly into a jar or crock. Pour in hot brine. Seal the container for long-term storage. Leave in a warm place. It will be ready to eat in five to seven days. It is delicious as a tangy pickle, great for stew or stir fry. Mustard greens are a versatile vegetable that keep well in the refrigerator.

Spicy Tofu in Tomatoes and Herb Sauce

MY MOTHER COOKED THIS DISH A LOT WHEN WE WERE GROWING up. IT's nothing fancy, but it is a staple, tasty and full of nutrition. Although I now have all sorts of sophisticated ways to prepare tofu, this recipe has remained one of my favorites. Sometimes I add vegetables, such as chunks of chayote squash, cut up string beans, or even carrots, which all work well with the tomato sauce.

1 lb. extra firm tofu cut into cubes, drain, dry with paper towel

Mix in bag:
Salt to taste or ½ tsp.
¼ tsp. black pepper
pinch of cayenne
1 tsp. granulated garlic
1 T. corn starch or rice powder

Add tofu to spice bag and shake well

Step Two:
2-3 T. minced shallot or ½ c. chopped onion
1 can (14 oz.) crushed tomatoes
½ t. hot pepper flake (optional)
1-2 T. fish sauce or soy sauce
½ c. broth or water
1-2 tsp. sugar, depending on the tartness of the tomatoes

Garnish:
½ c. mixed scallion and cilantro

Use just enough oil to create a thin coat on a large non-stick skillet and brown tofu on all sides. Remove and set aside.

In the same skillet, stir fry shallots until fragrant. Add the rest of the ingredients in Step Two. Bring to a boil. Return tofu to the skillet. Mix well to coat in sauce and simmer for seven to 10 minutes. Sprinkle with scallion and cilantro. Top with fresh ground black pepper. It would be a crime to serve this dish with anything other than rice.

Tips: Wait until the skillet gets very hot before drizzling oil and do not add herbs until the pan has been removed from heat. This dish can be made ahead of time. Like any braised dish, the taste will improve with time.

Spicy Tofu in Tomato and Herb Sauce

My Chicken Legs

My Chicken Legs

SHE WAS OUR HOUSEKEEPER IN SAIGON, EVEN THOUGH SHE WAS ONLY A few years older than I. She was the one who taught me about the birds and bees, not my Mom or Dad. Vietnamese parents don't discuss sex with their children. To me she was the older sister I never had. We talked about boys. We shared laughs and made fun of each other.

Even though I envied her tiny waist, every time we fought, I would say something like "who the heck would want you because of your abnormal waistline." She would come back with, "And who would want your skinny chicken legs." In my young mind, I expected her to stay with us so we could fight forever.

One day she took me aside and broke the news that she was leaving. I was stunned, horrified. I reminded her that she got a home with us and paid every month. I asked her why she wanted to take the risk and leave. Her answer has stayed with me. "Sometimes, in order to get somewhere, you have no choice but taking a risk."

We didn't see each other again for nearly 10 years. I walked into a little shop, like a mini market, and I was overwhelmed with joy to find out she was the owner, married, with kids, and she still had that tiny little waist I've only ever dreamed about. I couldn't help but take a shot at that. She came back right away with a question. "Where have your chicken legs taken you all these years? A little bird told me you left home." I grinned. "Someone told me that, sometimes, in order to get somewhere, you have no choice but to take a risk," I said. "That's just what I did."

There is nothing skinny about these chicken legs. They are plum full of goodies. They take a little time to prepare, but the taste is well worth the effort.

My Chicken Legs

4 whole legs, or 8 drumsticks

Remove the meat from the bone. Turn the meat inside out. Prepare the spices in a large bowl.

> 1 T. light soy sauce
> ½ tsp. salt
> ½ tsp. sugar
> ¼ tsp. black pepper
> ¼ tsp. cayenne pepper
> 1 T. vegetable oil

Mix well and rub paste all over the meat. Cover. Refrigerate at least two hours, or overnight. Make the filling:

> 1 lb. lean ground pork
> ¼ c. minced onion
> 2 T. crushed garlic
> 1 T. tapioca flour
> 1 T. creamy peanut butter
> 1 egg white
> 1 T. fish sauce (or soy sauce)
> ½ tsp. sugar
> ½ tsp. freshly crushed black pepper
> ¼ c. mix fresh cilantro and mint, minced

Mix well. Stuff the filling into the boneless pieces of chicken leg or drumstick. Lay in a roasting pan in a single layer. Roast in the oven at 350 degrees for one hour and 15 minutes for whole legs, 45 minutes to one hour for drumsticks.

Serve with mango chutney (see sauces in this book).

*Tip: To make the filling even better, sauté onion until brown. Add garlic. Cook until fragrant. Cool. Then add the onion and garlic to the rest of the filling ingredients.

Autumn in Paris

HER NAME WAS THU, WHICH TRANSLATES INTO ENGLISH AS AUTUMN. WE were good friends. I told her more than once how much I envied her because she was an only child and I was the oldest of eight.

Her father worked for the government. One summer, his job moved their family from Saigon to Paris. The week before they left, I would jump onto my bike and peddle over to her house every chance I got. I guessed her father held an important job, because they lived in a very nice house with servants and a cook who impressed me with her chicken curry.

We vowed to keep in touch. I should have known that it would be a fantasy, because the mail system at the time was costly and not reliable. Despite all odds, we did keep it going for a while. The last post card I got from her that fall was a picture of a little girl sitting under a beautiful, bright red apple tree.

Heaven knows how many times I've dreamed of sitting under that same tree with my friend.

Autumn in Paris Chicken

One:
¼ c. minced shallot (or ½ c. onion)
2 T. minced garlic
2 tsp. hot pepper flake (optional)
2-3 T. curry powder (depending on the brand or if it's home made)

Two:
2 lb. boneless chicken breast cut into cubes
1 tsp. sugar
2 tsp. salt
½ tsp. cayenne pepper
2 T. cornstarch

Three:
　　6 c. water (or broth) plus two bay leaves
　　10 c. of vegetables of your choice or:
　　2 c. potatoes cubed
　　2 c. string beans (approximately), cut in half
　　2 c. carrot cubed
　　4 c. sweet potatoes cubed

Four:
　　1 can coconut milk (13.5 oz.)
　　¼ c. cilantro

In a heated, large, heavy, non-stick skillet, place 2 T. canola oil and add the herbs and spices listed in step one. Sauté until fragrant. Add the ingredients listed in step two. Cook for three to five minutes, stirring constantly. Transfer everything to a Dutch oven and add the broth (or water). When it starts to boil, add the vegetables. Cook until the vegetables are tender, but still firm (10 to 15 minutes). Add the coconut milk and cilantro. Remove from heat.

This dish improves with time. It's great to make it ahead of time and let it sit for a day (in the refrigerator, of course), before serving it at dinner.

To serve: Reheat almost to boiling. Ladle it into a deep dish or shallow soup bowl. Sprinkle with fresh sliced hot pepper, like serano, Thai Dragon or Jalapeno. Serve with jasmine rice or sliced, crispy French bread.

Tips: Broth will definitely be the best choice. If you use water, add a bouillon cube to enhance the taste. (If you use bouillon, cut down on the salt in the recipe). Add vegetables according to density. For example, green beans take longer to cook than sweet potatoes.

Pork Loin for a Rainy Day

I REMEMBER THE BIRTHS OF MY YOUNGER BROTHERS AND SISTERS WITH fondness, not necessarily because they joined the family, but because of one dish the hospital served to new mothers—a salty, spicy pork dish. My mother would always share hers with me, and I savored every bite. To this day, I count this dish on my "comfort food" list. When it's raining, give me a few pieces of this pork, a bowl of hot and sour shrimp or fish soup, a big bowl of rice, and heaven is in my reach.

2 lbs. of whole pork loin, cut into thin slices (across whole loin)

Mix well with
1 T. shallot oil
1 T. white sugar
¼ c. brown sugar
¼ c. fish sauce
1 tsp. salt
1-2 tsp. freshly ground black pepper
2 tsp. crispy shallot

In a heavy-bottomed pan, carmelize the sugar. When the sugar is nicely brown, add the fish sauce and salt. Lower heat so the sugar can be dissolved. Put in the meat. Mix well with sauce and bring to a boil. Lower heat. Cover. Simmer for about 20 minutes, stirring occasionally. Add the ground pepper and crispy shallots after removing the pan from heat.

Spicy Braised Beef

THE SIBLING NEXT IN LINE TO ME IS MY SISTER, BICH NGOC. HER NAME translates into English as Blue Jade. Like a lot of sisters, we were always in conflict, maybe it was because we were so close in age. Probably the only time we'd agree on anything was when our mother took a day off from a hot stove and sent us to pick up some beef stew from a neighborhood restaurant. We would chat all the way and take turns carrying the food home. That was the only time she was sweet!

For years I have made this recipe when I'm rushed for time with harvesting duties in the fall garden. I prepare this dish, pack it in the slow cooker, and set the timer on the bread machine. When everybody is home from school and work, dinner is ready. Now-a-days the two oldest girls are in college. Although there are only three of us at home, I still make this dish, only four or five times bigger quantities. I take it to the market and share it with my friends and customers.

2 lbs. of stew beef or chuck, cut into cubes

Paste:
In a blender or food processor, combine the following:
2 Mexican chilies (hot or mild), soaked (reserve the liquid)
1 T. ginger
1 T. sugar
1 ½ tsp. salt
2 T. shallot
3 T. garlic
1 tsp. cinnamon
2 tsp. curry
1 tsp. star anise powder

Use ½ of the paste. Mix well into the beef. Let it rest. When you prep the vegetables, you'll need approximately four cups of cut up vegetables, such as potatoes, carrots, zucchini, string beans, etc.

In a Dutch oven with 1 T. canola oil, sauté the other half of the spice paste with 3 oz. of tomato paste. Then add four cups of broth or water, along with your reserved pepper liquid. Bring to a boil.

In a hot wok with 2 T. canola oil, sear the beef until it is aromatic. Remove the beef from the wok to the Dutch oven. This step is important, so do it in two or three batches. You don't want the beef to get watery. When meat and broth start to boil, lower the heat. Simmer for about an hour and a half. Add vegetables and 3-4 T. fish or soy sauce. Cook until the vegetables are tender, according to your own taste. I like my vegetables tender, but firm. It only takes 20 minutes to reach this state. My favorite vegetable mix for this is potatoes, carrots and leeks.

Rainy Days and Mondays (Never Get me Down) With my Mother's Buffalo and Water Spinach

It always rained in Vietnam. Rain would go on for days and days, non-stop. There were no televisions. I wonder now how my siblings and I entertained ourselves. We were never bored. When we got sick of being inside, we went outside to play under that warm and comfortable rain.

Food tastes so much better on rainy days, for some reason. We had a little pond in front of our house where my mother grew her water spinach.

It's still true. If you want something good to eat, you had better grow it yourself. Water spinach was fairly fresh if you bought it at the market, but it usually wasn't picked until it had grown to a large size. At our pond, we picked the water spinach when it had side shoots of about two inches. It is much smaller than regular spinach.

My mother had a special way to stir fry this vegetable. She would pick up a handful of the spinach and crush it lightly between both hands, using a rubbing motion. With plenty of fresh garlic, she would stir fry the water spinach with slices of tender water buffalo, which was a great deal cheaper than beef. Finding water buffalo, however, in the States might be a problem. Where would you even look? If you did find some, no doubt you would find it would be a lot more expensive than beef.

Hot Beef over Spinach

1 lb. flank steak, sliced thin
1 T. oil (shallot, garlic or vegetable)
1 tsp. sugar
½ tsp. black pepper
1 T. soy sauce
1 tsp. cayenne pepper

Mix well. Set aside. Blanch 1 lb. of washed spinach in boiling water for 30 seconds and let it drain. Then set the spinach into a large deep bowl.

Sauce:
1 T. rice wine vinegar
1 T. fish or soy sauce
1 T. oyster sauce
1 T. hoisin or brown sugar
1-3 T. your favorite hot sauce

In wok at high heat, sear beef, a few pieces at a time. Drizzle in oil, if needed. Arrange beef over the drained spinach.

Slice 1 large red onion
Mince 2 T. garlic

Once the beef is cooked, add a bit more oil to the wok, then cook onion and garlic for 2-3 minutes. Add the sauce. Bring to a boil, then pour over the beef and spinach. Like all quick cooking processes, it's best to serve this dish at once. Serves 4.

More Fish in the Sea

AT THE MARKET THERE WAS A FISH SECTION, A PLACE I STILL SOMETIMES see in my dreams. Beautiful fresh water fish, all shapes and sizes, swam in the big tank. There were large frogs, tied together by the belly into bunches. Golden eels twirled around inside a huge tub. I loved watching prawns as big as lobsters, or some as small as the tip of a pinky, jumping and dancing under a bright sun. Everything was still alive when we purchased it. That was the way of life. In this part of the world, fish was very popular because it was the cheapest. The average family consumed fish at least four times a week.

I loved my mother's best friend almost as much as my Mom. They called each other "Sister." She was married to an alcoholic. Whenever I visited, he would be sitting alone in the kitchen, which was separated from the main house. He would drink until he passed out at the table. Before his head hit the table, though, he would swear, curse and pick at her and their four kids.

One day, he brought home a woman, a younger version of his wife, and announced that she was his mistress and that she would be living with them.

They lived out in the countryside, about an hour's drive from Saigon, in a big house, surrounded by a beautiful tropical fruit orchard. I hated having to leave that place and head back into the city. My heart ached to leave that beautiful place.

The wife often took me to the market, to point out and explain how to pick a good chicken, how to get fresh fish by looking into its eyes, and how to dicker with vendors for the best buy. Her advice has stayed with me to this day.

When I got a little older, I remember asking her why she allowed her husband's mistress to live under the same roof. She said, "I'm grateful that she has taken over my duties with him." For a long time, I thought she meant cooking his dinner.

White Fish with Kohlrabi

WHEN THIS DISH IS COOKING OVER THE STOVE, IT HAS THE MAGIC POWER to take me all the way back to my childhood in Vietnam. This is one sample of classic northern Vietnamese cuisine.

In a large plastic bag, shake together:
1 ½ lb. of any firm white fish, cut into 2 inch cubes
1 tsp. salt
½ tsp. black pepper
1 T. corn starch
½ tsp. cayenne pepper (optional)

The aromatic:
¼ c. vegetable oil
½ c. thinly sliced shallot or onion
2 T. minced garlic

The sauce:
1 can crushed tomatoes (15 oz. or 4 large fresh, cut into chunks)
1 c. broth or 1 bottle of clam juice
1 tsp. sugar
2-3 T. fish sauce
1 c. freshly chopped dill
½ c. scallion, cut into 1 inch pieces
4 medium kohlrabi, cut into small chunks (equivalent to 2-3 cups)

In a large non-stick skillet, add oil. Brown the fish slightly. Be gentle and shake pan to prevent the fish from breaking up. Remove the fish and set aside.

Add the shallot to your heated pan and stir fry until shallot lightly brown. Add garlic and cook about 30-40 seconds, then add tomatoes, broth, sugar, fish sauce and kohlrabi. Mix well. Cover for 3-4 minutes. The timing is important. When the kohlrabi is half cooked, return the fish to the pan. Arrange it in the middle, in a single layer, so it can absorb the sauce evenly. This is the star of this dish. The first supporting role is the tomatoes. Next the kohlrabi and the herbs all add their special abilities to create harmony.

Cook for 3-4 more minutes, or just until kohlrabi is tender, but still firm and the fish is easily broken with a fork. Scatter in the herbs and freshly ground black pepper. Serve with plenty of rice. Serves 4-6.

My Mother

SHE'S A GENEROUS PERSON, WITH FEW WORDS TO SAY. BUT, WHEN SHE speaks, people around her have no choice but to listen. Her tiny body belies her internal strength. When my father left Vietnam for Philadelphia in April 1975 (shortly after I left), he took just one of my sisters with him. My mother was left behind with the rest of the brothers and sisters, whom she raised by herself. Our family wasn't reunited for more than 10 years.

Sometimes, when nobody is around, and all I have to do is cook a relaxing dinner just for the family, I can still hear the culinary advice of my mother, my teacher.

My Mother's Steamed Fish

2 slices of halibut—or your favorite firm white fish (1-1 ½ lb.)
1 oz. bean thread, soaked in warm water and drained
2 medium tomatoes, sliced

Sauce:
2 T. brown miso or soy sauce
1 T. chili garlic sauce (less if desired)
2 T. oyster sauce
½ tsp. black pepper
2 tsp. sesame oil

¼ c. sliced scallion

In a deep dish, which can easily fit into your wok or steamer, lay bean thread.

In a large bowl, whisk sauce until well blended. Coat fish with sauce, then lay it over the bean thread. Arrange tomatoes over the fish. Scatter scallion over the top.

With spatula, clean the rest of the sauce out of your bowl and drizzle it over the tomatoes. Steam over high heat, approximately 30-40 minutes. (Or, you may cover your baking dish with aluminum foil and bake in a 350 degree oven for 45 minutes.) Serve at once.

White Fish Dressed in Tuxedo, page 54

White Fish Dressed in Tuxedo

LOOK AT THE INGREDIENTS WE USE HERE. NOTHING BUT THE BEST FOR your health! But that's just a bonus point, because you'll keep coming back to this recipe for the taste. If you have never used miso before, at least try it this once.

Normally, I would love to do this dish with the whole fish—head and tail still attached. Where I live right now, however, it is almost impossible to find one, so I just have to use fillet.

> 1 lb. of halibut, haddock or any white fish, cut into 4 pieces
> 1 lb. of firm tofu, cut crosswise into 4 slices
> 8 oz. sliced white button mushrooms
> 8 dried black shiitake mushrooms, soaked

> **White miso paste:**
> 4-6 T. white miso paste
> 2 tsp. sugar
> 1 T. garlic oil
> 1 T. shallot oil
> A dash of sesame oil
> 1 tsp. white pepper
> ¼ c. mirin (sweet Japanese sake)

In a medium-sized bowl, mix paste until smooth. Use half for the fish. Rub the sauce evenly over each piece, then lay the fish in an oven-proof casserole or deep oval plate. Rub tofu with the rest of the miso paste. Alternate the slices with the fish. Cover with white mushrooms. Use the black shiitake and decorate like a tuxedo. Cover the dish with foil.

In the middle of the wok, place a medium sized stainless steel bowl—or rack, if you have one—and situate the fish dish on top. Pour in water until at least two inches comes up the outside of the fish casserole dish. Set heat at high and steam for 20-25 minutes.

Chicken Soup with Rice and Herbs

WE MET AT THE PLAYGROUND. I LIKED HER BUBBLY PERSONALITY immediately. We were the same age, but she was much smaller than I. She invited me to visit her house, so I followed her home one day, down the end of that small dirt road, over on the other side of town.

When I saw her sister rinse rice out of a pot, I asked what she was doing. "I'm cooking rice soup," she said. Without thinking, I said, "Gee, I don't know why any body would want to eat gooey rice soup when they can eat a nice fluffy bowl of rice."

My friend answered me, with a lot less bubbling in her voice, "That's all the rice we have, so if we make soup, then each of us can have a bowl."

That was one of the first lessons I learned, and it wasn't just about rice. Her house was one room with a dirt floor. I had seen poverty before, when I walked to and from school. The route took me through an expensive neighborhood, with streets lined with mansions. Then there were shacks—bamboo huts with dirt floors. I swore I'd never live in such a house. My parents' house had a shiny tile floor. My best friend, who was 18, lived next door. She had all the latest Western stuff—Elvis, Fats Domino, Bridget Bardot magazines. Her father was a doctor. Her mother was his mistress. My world got turned upside down when my family went bankrupt. We left the house with the shiny tile floor and moved to a smaller house with a cement floor. I lost my best friend in the move. I was traumatized. I was so angry with my parents. After we moved away, my best friend died of a lung disease. Her untimely death fueled my anger toward my parents.

Chicken Soup with Rice and Herbs

1 large roaster (5-6 lbs., rinsed)
4-5 quarts of water
1 ¼ c. jasmine or long grain rice
3 oz. ginger, crushed
¼ c. fish sauce
1 tsp. salt

In a large soup pan, add all the above ingredients. Bring to a gentle boil for 1 ½ hours. Remove chicken. Let it cool slightly, then pull all the meat off the bones by hand, shredding it into bite-size pieces. Remove all bones and skin. Skim off all visible fat from your broth. Return the shredded meat to the soup. Add ½ c. scallions, cut into ¼ inch pieces and ½ c. cilantro leaves, chopped.

This soup has a shelf life of 4-5 days in the refrigerator. It's good as is, or great if you add a handful of fresh bean sprouts, a teaspoon of freshly chopped hot peppers and a touch of freshly squeezed lemon juice.

Rice

IN VIETNAM, RICE COMES IN A LOT OF VARIETIES, BUT WHEN I WAS growing up there were only a few choices that I knew and liked—long grain, short grain, glutinous, red and broken. Rice is such an important part of the culture that we greeted one another in Vietnam by saying "Have you eaten your rice today?" (Okay, so we borrowed the greeting from the Chinese, but, hey, what do you expect? The Chinese were part of our culture for a thousand years. We were bound to pick up a few Chinese ideas.)

Jasmine scented rice cost more, so long grain was what we usually ate for dinner. Sweet rice, or glutinous rice, is breakfast rice. Red rice and broken rice are lower grades; therefore, they are cheaper.

The big question is, when to serve white rice and when to serve fried rice? Fried rice goes well with light main dishes, in some ways balancing them. Dishes with heavier seasoning and sauces are better accompanied by white rice.

Always use cold or cooled rice to make fried rice. If you use hot rice, the rice will stick to your wok and you will end up making mush rice. When it's an emergency, I dry cooked hot rice with a fan or spread it in a deep cookie pan, then put it in the freezer for 10 to 15 minutes. I prefer to serve jasmine rice with just about any dish. Well seasoned fried rice is a meal by itself, and it should be enjoyed as it is.

Rice feeds more people around the globe than any other grain. Therefore, it is safe to say I'm not the only one addicted to this little grain.

Basic Sweet Rice

SWEET RICE, GLUTINOUS OR STICKY RICE, IS THE SAME NAME FOR OPAQUE rice grain. Before the invention of the microwave, I used to have to soak it overnight, then steam it the next day. God bless the modern era. Here's my short cut version. From here, you can go anywhere.

> 1 ¼ c. sweet rice
> 6 c. hot tap water
> Cover, soak for 2 hours. Drain.

Put rice in a microwave proof dish with lid, pour in 2 cups boiling water. Microwave on high heat for 8-10 minutes. Stir once. Let it rest for 5 minutes.

Hot Sour Fish Soup

I WAS EATING A BOWL OF SOUP WHEN I LEARNED THAT PRESIDENT NGO Dinh Diem and his brother had been killed by their own army on that November day in 1963. It's funny how food can become associated in your memory with sad or happy times. I had met the Vietnamese president while I was on an elementary school field trip when he was still new in the job. We had been told to stand beside the road and wave the flag. That was all we had to do, and that's all we knew. He got out of the black car a little distance from where I stood. I saw him rub some kid's head, and then, there he was, right in front of me, smiling down. I was struck by the kindness of his eyes. I heard him say something, and I tried to say something, but I was sort of mumbling when I reached out my hand. He shook my hand in a gentle squeeze. He touched a few more hands down the road, got back in the car and that was it for us. Even at that young age, I could sense the power of his presence.

Hot Sour Fish Soup with Vegetables

2-3 T. canola oil
4-5 cloves garlic
½ tsp. hot pepper flakes
1 lb. white fish, cut into large cubes
8-10 cups broth

Seasoning:
¼ c. fish sauce
1 tsp. salt
2 tsp. sugar
1 T. concentrated Tamarind paste or 3 T. white vinegar

Vegetables:
2 c. cut up, fresh tomatoes, or 1 14 oz. can
2 c. julienne cut cabbage
1 lb. fresh or frozen okra
2 c. bean sprouts

Garnish:
¼ c. scallion, chopped
½ c. French mint, or 2 tsp. cumin
2-5 fresh hot pepper, thinly sliced

In soup pan with 2 T. of oil, brown fish with garlic and hot pepper. Remove and set aside. Pour in broth. Bring broth to boil. Add vegetables. Simmer until vegetables are tender, but crisp. Return the fish to the pan. Add seasonings. Cook just until fish is easily flaked with a fork. Remove from heat and add garnish. Serve. This is an excellent companion dish to Rainy Day Pork Loin and a bowl of jasmine rice.

Not All Coconuts Created Equal

When I was a teenager, I wanted to be a singer. I got an audition at the most famous music school in Saigon—our Julliard. Everyone who graduated from there became big stars. My parents never knew. I figured if I got in I would surprise them with the news. This was my deal. I knew I would need help. I found out where a famous music teacher lived. I pedaled my bike out to where he lived—three hours away. I had three weeks to prepare. I begged him to teach me. He didn't want to see me, because I couldn't pay. But, I told him that I could pay him when I was famous. He agreed to coach me. I went three times a week.

On the day of the audition, all the hopefuls gathered in a big auditorium. There was a huge, overwhelming audience. I watched as others performed and thought I could do better. My name was called. On my way to the stage, I overheard some guys making jokes about my breasts—"Look at those two coconuts." I was humiliated. When the music started, I missed the beat. My face was burning hot. Needless to say, I didn't get in to the school. My dream went bust.

Sweet Rice with Coconut and Toasted Sesame

THIS WAS MY CHILDREN'S BREAKFAST FOOD UNTIL THEY SPROUTED WINGS to fly away from home. If you have any left over steamed mung beans stored in the freezer, get them out.

> 1 basic sweet rice recipe and 1 tsp. salt
> 1 c. cooked mung bean (optional)
> 1 c. fresh grated coconut
> ¼ c. sugar
> ¼ c. toasted, crushed sesame seed
> ¼ tsp. salt

Prepare sweet rice. Stir in bean at half time. In a small bowl, mix together sugar, sesame and salt.

To serve: In a medium bowl with 1 cup rice, sprinkle in 1-2 T. grated coconut and 1-2 tsp. sugar and sesame salt. Serve warm or at room temperature.

A word about sugar: Sugar plays a crucial part in most cases. It enhances the taste or helps tenderize meat. But if it's an issue, you may substitute whatever you are comfortable with. You may use date sugar instead of what I've listed, for example.

Chapter Two

ON MY OWN

On My Own

WHEN I WAS EIGHTEEN, I APPLIED FOR AN I.D. CARD SO I COULD GET A job, then I ran away from home. In Vietnam, unmarried children always remained at home with their parents. This, of course, caused a big stir in our family, but just like any other shock, it wore off with the passage of time. I was a rebel. I didn't like all the rules and regulations my parents (mostly my Mom) had.

I struggled between jobs, sometimes having to go days without food. I was homeless for a while, staying with friends for a few days at a time. If you ever walked through the food court off Le Loi Boulevard in Saigon City, you will understand this story.

One afternoon I was out looking for a job. I can't remember why I ended up in that part of town. I guess it was the aroma of beef soup calling out to my empty stomach. The only thing I can recall was the fragrant aroma of Siam Queen basil, which cut through my brain like a razor. The next thing I knew, I was waking up in some sort of powder room, with a cold towel on my head.

Soon enough I learned I had been found unconscious in front of a tea bar, a typical type of club all over the South of Vietnam at that time. The girls who worked at such places made their living by drinking what they called "Saigon tea," and by chatting with customers, most of whom were young, lonely U.S. soldiers. The more tea you drank, the more money you would make. Lucky for me, the club needed someone in the kitchen, so I was hired.

That was my first decent job, the beginning of my journey. I still believe that things happen for a reason.

Her club name was Lee Ann. (Each of the girls took an American name in the club.) After she found out that I was homeless, she took me in until I got my first paycheck. I felt lucky for the generosity she offered. She was a year older than I, married to her childhood/neighbor sweetheart. They had a little boy, two years old.

In the weeks that followed, we developed a relationship. We shared cabs to work, we shared cooking and cleaning responsibilities at home, and we shared "girl talk." I liked my new friend and her son very much, but I hated her husband. The guy was bossy, cruel with words and insanely jealous.

I guess I had a low opinion of him from the start, because, if I had been a man, I would never have allowed my wife to work in that sort of place where the job description was flirting, kissing, and, quite often, having sex with the customer. When I expressed my dismay to her, she defended him by explaining to me that it was only a temporary arrangement, until they saved enough money for him to start a business. "Besides," she said, "I only drink tea to make money. I don't have sex with the clients."

Then one day, I saw her walk out of the bar with a handsome G.I. I knew who he was. She had been talking to me about him for days. We usually talked in the cab on our way back to her house. Once there, the conversation would change to anything but what happened at the bar.

I knew she was quite fond of young Willy. According to her, he smelled good, he was a good kisser, and he treated her like a princess.

The day she left the club with Willy, the conversation in the cab was pointed. I was upset with her. I asked if she had been paying Willy with sex for his kindnesses. "I thought you didn't do that stuff," I said. She was crying. "He's going home, you know. I didn't do it for the money. I really like him."

The next day at work, around noon, her husband walked in and went straight to the table where she sat with a customer. He dragged her out of the club. By the time I got back to her house, she wasn't there. Someone told me she was in the hospital. When I saw her there, she looked like a bloody rag doll.

Her husband had so severely beaten her that she would never be able to have another child.

How had he found out? He had been reading my diary since I moved in. My words helped put my friend in the Intensive Care Unit.

Vung Tau Chili Crab

IN THE SUMMER OF 1968, I TOOK A VACATION TO THE BEACH WITH MY roommate Hong (Rose). We took the bus. It took forever. The Viet Cong would shoot artillery at the road traffic. But, when we got there, there was no war at the beach. It was so peaceful. It was like there were two different worlds. I think the previous danger on the road made the feelings even more intense.

I always remember how overwhelmed I felt when I saw the ocean for the first time, there, at that beach. I can still taste the Chili Crab at *Vung Tau* beach that summer. I sat in a wooden chair under an umbrella, with a big bowl in my hand full of this sweet salty spicy crab. In that moment, the whole world stood still and was perfect.

I have cooked this dish from time to time, but I haven't felt that intense feeling again. It was a one time deal, I guess.

4 fresh crabs*

Process into a paste:
4 hot chilies
6 large cloves garlic
1 piece of ginger, big as your thumb (1/2 inch)

Mix:
2 T. tomato paste or ketchup
3 T. sugar
1 tsp. salt
1 tsp. hot sauce
1 T. fish sauce
¼ c. water broth or claim juice

3-4 T. oil
2 beaten eggs
¼ c. scallion cut into ½ inch pieces

Remove crab shell and unwanted parts. Cut each crab into fourths. Using a large knife, lightly crush the claws, legs, and body without making it fall apart.

In a hot wok, swirl in oil and fry the spice paste until fragrant. Add crab pieces and stir fry for 3 to 5 minutes. Stir in sauce. Mix well. Cover. Cook for 4 to 5 minutes. Take the lid off. Pour in egg. Swirl around until egg is cooked thoroughly. Toss in scallion and serve. This is great with good company and frosty margaritas.

*You may substitute frozen Alaskan king crab legs for the fresh crab. Thaw. Chop into two-three inch strips and prepare the sauce. Toss together and enjoy the simple pleasures.

The Other Red Meat

It was a celebrity garden party. People were dressed up. There was lavish food. We were surrounded by beautiful flowers and tropical fruit trees. My kind of fun. I happily skipped all the small talk (i.e., gossip), and went straight for the food.

Somebody was grilling under a guava tree. Nothing grabs my attention quicker than the aroma of grilled food. I love just about anything that has been marinated and grilled, or so I thought. As I approached, someone offered me a plate of grilled stuffed meat in grape leaves. My mother used to make this dish, using ground pork and *xuong xong* leaves. As a popped a little log into my mouth, all I noticed was the aroma; however, as I crunched into the filling, the texture of the meat took me off guard. Just before I was about to swallow, I asked the cook, "What kind of meat is it?"

He gave me a look, like, "what planet are you from?" "It's dog. Isn't it great?" he said. Believe me, I didn't need to hear anything else he had to say. I spat whatever I had in my mouth into my hand. I walked away. I didn't even bother to apologize for the noise I made clearing out my throat. You can only imagine what I went through the first time I saw hot dogs at the supermarket.

Hamburger Not-so-basics

IF GROUND DOG ISN'T YOUR FAVORITE, TRY SOME GROUND BEEF. HERE are some ideas with which you can turn ground beef into something special.

Everyday Dress Up Burger

1 lb. ground round
½ tsp. black pepper
½ tsp. salt
1 T. oyster sauce
Mix well. Pan fry, broil or grill.

Banquet Burger

1 lb. ground round
½ tsp. white pepper
1 T. light soy sauce
1 T. oyster sauce
1 tsp. sesame oil
2 T. rice wine
1 T. granulated garlic
¼ c. chopped scallion.

I recommend grilling these burgers.

Vietnamese Flair

1 lb. ground sirloin
1 T. minced garlic
1 T. fish sauce
¼ tsp. black pepper
¼ t. salt

1-10 fresh hot peppers, like Birds Eye or Thai Dragon, minced
2 T. lemongrass, finely chopped
1 tsp. caramel (See Sauces and Garnishes)
¼ c. chopped scallion

Mix well. Divide into four burgers. Grill over hot coals. This is a special treat. Serve this with Cole Slaw (pg. 31) and rice, instead of on a bun.

Beef with Rice Noodles and Basil

THIS SOUP IS VERY POPULAR WITH MY FAMILY, AS WELL AS WITH MY sophisticated customers. There is a life time of memories with this dish. On very special days, when I was a child, we got to go to a nearby restaurant in our neighborhood and have a bowl of this soup. I savored the food and the company of my family.

When I was older and out in the work place, I had a friend married to a well known actor. Through them, I got to know a bit about the inside of the entertainment business in Vietnam. I hung out with celebrities and dated a few. There was a famous restaurant in Saigon which specialized in this soup. We were there a lot—weekend, week day—it didn't matter. I have to admit that was the most fun and freest time of my life. We ate out a lot.

I didn't start to make this soup until I moved to Maine. One look around, and I realized that if I didn't start to cook, I would go hungry.

I provide two versions of this dish. The long one is definitely better, but if you don't have time, go with the short cut. It works for me when I don't feel liking making a fuss.

For the broth:
  4-5 lbs. combination of bones (short ribs and ox tail, washed, rinsed)
  4-5 lbs. round roast, washed, rinsed
  1 lb. carrots, cut into chunks
  5-6 star anise
  3 oz. ginger, charred over flame until golden brown, crushed
  1 large onion charred over flame until black spots appear
  ¼ c. fish sauce
  1 stick cinnamon
  1-2 T. salt

Put all the above ingredients in a large stock pot. Cover with water, plus 4-5 inches above the top of the bones. Bring to a boil over medium heat. After approximately 2 hours, take out the roast, then lower heat to the lowest setting and simmer for another 2 hours. At this point, the meat will fall off the bone. Keep the meat, discard the bones and spices. Skim off the fat and strain broth through layers of cheese cloth to get rid of the impurities. This step is not important unless you want to impress your guests with a clear broth. This process can be done 1-2 days ahead.

For the presentation:
Slice the roast into ribbons of 2"x3" medium thin
1 bunch fresh cilantro
1 bunch scallions, cut into ½ inch long pieces
1 medium sweet onion, sliced paper thin
freshly ground black pepper
1 lb. medium wide flat rice noodles, soaked for ½ hour (plunge these into boiling water for 2-3 minutes, drain, rinse thoroughly with cold water). This step can be done early and the noodles can be refrigerated until needed.

For accompaniments:
Fresh bean sprouts (2-3 cups)
1-2 lime or lemon, cut into wedges
1 bunch of Thai basil, such as Siam Queen
hot chili sriracha
hoisin sauce
extra fish sauce
fresh hot pepper, such as Thai Dragon

To assemble:
In a large soup bowl, lay in order
Approximately 8 oz. cooked noodles
2-4 oz. sliced, cooked beef
handful combination of sliced onion, cilantro and scallion
freshly ground black pepper

Bring broth to boil and pour approximately 10-12 oz. of broth over layer of noodles, meat and serve with accompaniments. Before pouring in the broth, you may microwave the noodle bowl for 1-2 minutes for extra hot soup.

My favorite part is having a small bowl of the meat that has fallen off the bone. I dip the pieces one by one into hoisin and sriracha hot sauce. Leftovers freeze well. Serves 4-6.

Quick Beef Noodle Soup

1 lb. of rice noodles, cooked as described above
1 lb. of beef sirloin, sliced thin

Broth:
   2 cans beef broth
   1 can water
   1 oz. crushed ginger
   1-3 star anise
   dash cinnamon
   2 T. fish sauce

Bring broth to boil. Simmer for five minutes. Assemble soup as described above. The meat will cook as you pour in boiling broth. Serve with accompaniments. Serves 4.

Chapter Three

BIEN HOA

The New Journey

I left Saigon right after my friend from the tea club was beaten by her husband. I couldn't stand the thought of facing that man, especially after she chose to go back to him. I found a job as a cashier for a brand new officers club inside Bien Hoa Air Base.

The first day at Bien Hoa, I was excited. The club was owned by Vietnamese and Chinese business people. They treated us very well. The whole staff stayed in one big house, not too far away from the base. After I settled in, it was late, but my housemates and I decided to go in search of food. After we had eaten, we walked back to our house. Suddenly, out of nowhere, a police patrol stopped us.

Before we knew what was happening, we were pushed into a big police car and dumped at the local jail. We were convicted of violating the city's curfew. We were released the next morning. Food has gotten me into a lot of situations in my life. This time it had put me in a cage.

G.I. Blues

THE RAIN POURED DOWN NON-STOP THE FIRST FEW WEEKS I WORKED inside Bien Hoa. I had a habit of always coming in early. I liked to watch the G.I.s come and go from the unit next door to our club. My dressing room window provided a good view.

On that particular day, the young airman caught my eye. I noticed him as soon as he emerged from the building. He wasn't going any where. He just walked up and down, then turned around and did it all over again.

Even in the warm rain, somehow I could feel the chill of his loneliness. I was deep in my thoughts. Before I knew it, I was weeping for him. He was so young.

"What in the world is he doing here?" I asked myself. "Why does he have to be here, away from his family, maybe away from a young wife? Why did he have to get caught in all this?"

Suddenly, I had a strong urge to run into that rain just to tell that young man how much I appreciated him and his people who were sacrificing everything to help my country. But I didn't have the nerve to do it.

That was a turning point for me. I decided to make the trip to Saigon that week to make peace with my family, and I did.

Steamed Pork with Anchovy and Chilies

AFTER MAKING UP WITH MY FAMILY, I WOULD SOMETIMES GO AND VISIT and cook for them. As I mentioned earlier, my mother cooked mostly Northern style cuisine. She usually criticized the aroma of Southern food because it is—how shall I put this—odiferous. The following recipe is a Southern favorite. I learned it from the lady who cooked for the club where I worked at Bien Hoa. It is an ordinary dish, using simply ground pork, fermented fish and egg, then steamed and served with cold shredded cucumber. I cooked it a lot, especially when I visited my parents. As soon as my mother entered the house, she would take one whiff, and declare, "Nga is home."

Steamed Pork with Anchovy and Chilies

1 lb. ground pork
½ oz. bean vermicelli soaked in warm water, cut into 1 inch pieces
3 T. minced shallot
1 T. minced garlic
2 Thai hot chilies, minced
2 oz. anchovies, chopped
1 T. fish sauce
½ tsp. black pepper
1 tsp. sugar

3 eggs
garnish with diced scallion stalk and hot pepper

If you have a food processor, process all ingredients before adding meat. Mix meat and seasoning well before adding the egg. If you mix by hand, do the same.

Grease a loaf pan or 1 ½ quart casserole. Pour in mixture. Make sure your steam rack is in place in your wok. Put enough water into the bottom of the wok so that the water level comes up to the bottom of your loaf or casserole pan. Center your loaf pan or casserole on the steam rack. Put lid on wok. Steam over high heat for 40-50 minutes.

Serve with shredded cucumber and rice.

"Dear John"

RICHARD INTRODUCED ME TO THAT GOOD OL' AMERICAN STAPLE—THE pot roast. He was one of my many new friends I made at my new job after I left the officers' club at Bien Hoa. I was working for the United States now, which meant good pay, with even better tips. There was live music every night, which I enjoyed very much. And that's not all!

A gold mine came with the job. Everything sold at the PX was valuable outside the gate. Of course, I wasn't allowed to shop there, so I bought the merchandise from all my new friends, who were willing to shop for me. They could make some extra money, and, for a bonus, I cooked for them. It worked like a charm.

Richard was one of my good business associates. One day, Richard got a "Dear John" letter from his young wife. How could this be? This letter came from the same woman who had just a few days before sent him a card, which he proudly showed to everyone: "I miss you. I'm so lost without you."

My guess is that wherever she had been lost, she had found somebody else there.

It was early in the afternoon, but Richard was already drunk. He was screaming at somebody and smashing a huge watermelon against the mess hall's outside wall.

I watched my friend in his anguish. I couldn't help but feel overwhelmed with sadness. I also felt hatred toward his wife. How could I hate a woman I had never met?

He always called me a nut, then he would go on to muse, "Too bad you aren't my nut." I just laughed. I didn't want to know what that meant.

He was never the same person after the letter from "her." Near the end of his time in Vietnam, to express his gratitude for all the meals I'd fixed him, he volunteered to cook for me an American classic: pot roast. He made a pretty mean pot roast.

Spicy Pot Roast

EVERYONE HAS HIS OR HER OWN VERSION OF POT ROAST: A BIG CHUNK OF meat braised in liquid for a couple of hours. For that reason, you really can play with the ingredients to make one pot roast totally different from another. I can go on and on about this subject. Pot roast is one of my favorite comfort foods. Let's just say for the first cold day in the fall, I find myself going back to make this particular one.

Put 2 T. of vegetable oil into a Dutch oven. Add:
1 c. onion, quartered
1 bulb of garlic (Note: this is not one clove. A bulb contains several cloves.)
2-5 serano chilies, crushed
2 stalks lemongrass, crushed
3-4 lbs. beef roast (chuck, rump or round are all good)
1 can beef broth
1 c. of water
2 T. fish sauce
1 t. salt
1 T. dark soy sauce
4 pieces of crystallized ginger
4 oz. of sliced mushrooms

On high heat, sauté the first four ingredients. Center the roast in the middle. Pour in the next five ingredients. Bring to a boil, then cover and lower heat. Simmer from 1 ½ hours to 2 hours, depending on the desired tenderness. Let it sit for 10 to 20 minutes. Remove meat, slice and place onto serving plate. Strain juice. Pour over meat. Serve with rice and your favorite steamed vegetables. I generally choose cabbage and Brussels sprouts.

Tear Drop

HER NAME WAS LE, WHICH MEANS FAST, BUT WITH A HALF MOON MARK on the /e/, it means "tear drop." Some wise folks often said that whoever bore that name would most likely have a tragic life. I really don't believe that kind of lore, but in this case, it made me wonder.

The first time we met, we were at a private party in Saigon. In Vietnam, we don't have Halloween parties, but in the fall well-to-do people would throw parties to celebrate the moon with elaborate food, including whole roasted pig, or even a cow, over a big fire, with all the fixings and, of course, moon cake. Le and I were there with dates. I don't know the circumstances of her date, but mine was just a meal ticket. Once there, the guys mingled with other guests, and Le and I started talking to each other.

I learned she was an artist. It made a lot of sense, because she seemed to know everybody in the club business—song writers, singers, actors. She was very easy on the eyes—a Vietnamese Michelle Pfeiffer.

We had two things in common: we liked good food and we loved to make fun of the flaws of the male of the species. She lived in Saigon, so whenever I was in town, we would meet for dinner or shopping. She fixed me up with blind dates a few times, insisting that we not spend money in fancy restaurants. "Let somebody else pick up the bill," she said. The best part was that we would have someone to make fun of later.

In Vietnam, just because the guy buys dinner doesn't mean the woman is obligated to him in any way, just good clean fun.

This was the time I learned a lot about eating exotic foods, like shark fin soup, crispy rice over abalone, soup made with rare birds' spit. The guys who picked up the tabs were middle aged rich men. I asked her why she couldn't get us hooked up with someone younger and better looking. She said younger men were complicated and didn't have any money. These guys didn't expect anything other than our company. There weren't any emotional entanglements. She just wanted to have fun. I did, too, but I told her I also enjoyed girls' night out, so next time it was just going to be the two of us.

We went shopping, out to dinner, night clubbing at a coffee bar with live music. She invited me to stay over night at her apartment. When we got back to her place, it was late but she suggested we should have tea out on the balcony. (She lived on the second floor.)

In the middle of our tea, I saw a man get out of his car across the street. He could barely walk, he was so drunk. He looked right at us, screaming. In the middle of the night the air was still, and I heard every sharp word, even though he was slurring his speech. "You are a wicked whore! You cleaned me out, then you dumped me like a dirty rag! What makes you think you can get away with treating me like that?"

I asked her why he was looking at us. I asked her if she knew him. She hesitated for a second, then said. "No, but I have an idea who he's cursing at. It must be the call girl who lives upstairs. Let's go inside." Before the door closed his voice screeched in the dark night. "You are a dead whore! You hear me? Maybe I'll spare your life and toss acid in your pretty face, then no man will want to look at you again!" She seemed quiet after that. I remember the conversation we had that night.

I said I wondered why a woman would want to be in that kind of job. It must be money, I suggested. She said money was good, but that she didn't think that money was the only factor. She said she thought sometimes a woman who got her feelings hurt might just want to get revenge.

A couple of months later, after picking up some clothes from a tailoring shop in Saigon, I made an impromptu stop at her apartment just for a quick visit before I returned to Bien Hoa. I rang the door bell, but it wasn't my girl friend who opened the door. I asked for Tear Drop. The person who answered the door said he was really sorry, but that my friend had been killed three weeks before. "There was an accident right down the road," he said, pointing. "Hit and run, you know. The good thing is she died immediately. Her family came and collected her body and brought it back to the south." I also found out that she had a son.

They never found out who did it. I have a pretty good idea.

Two Times Chicken

2 whole breasts, boneless, with skin on
2 T. light soy sauce
1 T. mirin wine, rice wine or sherry
Mix the soy sauce and wine together and rub over both breasts. Set aside.

Stuffing:
1 lb. chicken breast, boneless, cut into cubes
¼ c. water chestnut
¼ c. shiitake mushroom or button mushroom
1 tsp. sesame oil
1 egg white
2 T. sweet mirin, rice wine or sherry
2 T. oyster sauce

Place the chicken cubes into a food processor. Pulse until the chicken is coarsely chopped. Remove to a bowl. Place mushroom and water chestnut in the food processor. Pulse until vegetable coarsely chopped. Add the vegetables to the chopped chicken. Add the remaining ingredients and mix well. Divide into two parts. Place on the reserved chicken breasts and spread evenly. Roll up each breast and secure with string.

Roast in the oven at 350 degrees for one hour and 15 minutes. Cool before slicing.

Two Times Chicken, page 89

Pork and Pineapple Fried Rice, page 92

Pork and Pineapple Fried Rice

When I worked at Bien Hoa airbase, I met and made friends with many people who have left warm memories in my heart. Billy was one of those people.

My boss, Wayne, introduced us. Wayne, who hailed from Hawaii, was round and short. He said he wanted me to meet his twin. He was my boss, so I said "sure," but I wasn't that enthusiastic.

Twins! I don't think it's possible for two people to be more different. Billy was tall and leggy. He had blue eyes guaranteed to melt any girl's heart. He was gorgeous. Wayne called him Billy Blue because of those blue eyes, the color of a deep ocean. He was a warm, charming man.

I only had one day a week off. Usually, on that day, I would travel to the base to spend time with Billy. We would meet at the bus stop. From there, he would take me to the officer's club for dinner. Sometimes, we would stay and enjoy a live band, but most of the time, we just went to the movies (25 cents a ticket). I still remember those films: *Butch Cassidy and the Sundance Kid; Two Mules for Sister Sarah; They Shoot Horses, Don't They.*

On our last date before he headed out to fly a mission, he asked me if I could make fried rice. I said, "Yes, in endless ways." I asked him if there was a particular dish he wanted. He said, pork and pineapple. "Piece of cake," I told him. I asked him what he was going to trade for the dish. "How about a trip to Hawaii?" he asked. "You've got a deal," I told him.

The day we were supposed to meet, I was edgy. There was a knot in my stomach for some reason, but I did make the fried rice. Then I went to our usual meeting place. While I sat at the bus stop, the rain, which had started earlier, started coming down more heavily, pounding against the little shelter where I sat. People came and went, but there was no sign of Billy. He had never been late before, but, I told myself, there's a first time for everything. I can't remember how long I sat there and waited for Billy Blue. Wayne finally came. All I had to do was look in his eyes, and I knew what had happened. I heard Wayne talking. I must have been cold, because my hand was shaking so bad that I couldn't hold on to the container. Rice and pineapple went everywhere. I felt like I was drowning. Wayne's voice seemed to be coming from far, far away. He was saying, "He told me before he left, he was going to take you to Hawaii to meet his Mom."

Pork and Pineapple Fried Rice

4 oz. lean, thinly sliced pork loin, mixed with ½ t. pepper and ½ t. salt
2 T. shallot, minced
1 T. garlic, minced
3-4 c. cooled, cooked rice
1 c. cubed, gold, sweet pineapple

Sauce:
1 T. oyster sauce
2 T. broth or water
1 T. ketchup
1-2 T. light soy sauce
1 tsp. hot sauce, such as sriracha (optional)
¼ c. green onion and cilantro

In a hot wok, with 2-3 tablespoons canola oil, sauté the shallots for 2 minutes. Add garlic. Stir for 30 seconds, then add pork. When the pork is brown in 2 to 3 minutes, add the rice. Toss to blend until heated through (2 to 3 minutes). Add a bit more oil if needed to prevent the rice from sticking. Swirl in stock. Add pineapple. When rice is hot to the touch, sprinkle in the herbs and serve.

*Tips: The key ingredient to good fried rice is the sauce taste. Adjust the soy sauce. You may need a little more or a little less to fit your taste buds. I like cilantro in this dish, but if you don't like cilantro, don't use it. I always use fresh pineapple. If fresh isn't available, one small can of chunk pineapple will do. Make sure to drain canned pineapple before you use it.

New Year 1968

I SHARED A HOUSE WITH THREE OTHER WOMEN WHEN I WORKED at BIEN Hoa Air Base. None of us wanted to face the chore of preparing breakfast, so we would go out to eat. Bien Hoa was a busy place for eateries. My roommates and I had a favorite place where we were treated like family. They offered delicious dumplings filled with chicken and the best black sesame pudding. We adored the people who owned the café. We called them, in Vietnamese, of course, Ma, Pa, bro and sis. They always gave us extra food, which, of course, made us feel special. I have remembered this with my own customers.

I remember one morning, as we walked toward our special café, talking about the explosion we had heard the night before. It had sounded like the rocket had hit right next door. Rocket explosions weren't unusual. We did, after all, live close to Bien Hoa Air Base, a target of the enemy.

We turned the corner toward the café, and saw before us—nothing. That part of town was vaporized, as though it had never existed.

As we walked away, dazed, I realized that their deaths were a blessing in a way. After all, they had died together. I couldn't have imagined being the only survivor. As we walked away, we talked about what we would eat if we knew it was our last meal. We talked about how our friends would have gone to bed the night before, not knowing that they had just eaten their last meal. One of my friends said she wouldn't be able to eat, knowing it to be her last meal. The rest of us decided we could and would.

The Unforgettable New Year

IT WASN'T UNTIL THE TET OFFENSIVE IN 1968 THAT THE WAR ACTUALLY became a reality for me. The day before Tet, I had just put my key into the lock of my apartment, when I heard the whine of a helicopter overhead, but it didn't sound right. It crashed only a half block away. I could see bodies exploding from the helicopter as it hit. A piece of burning metal hit the ground a couple of feet from where I was standing. The noise was incredible. It felt like it was under my rib cage. I couldn't breath from the pressure.

The next morning, the holiday, I got up and left the apartment to look for breakfast. The street was filled with people, running. They had their pets with them. They had everything they could carry. What happened, I asked a woman with a child in her arms and two more kids screaming right along side of her. "We lost it. They're here. They're here," she said.

They were there indeed, right before the eyes of Saigon City and many other places. For me and the rest of the city slickers, we learned the new meaning of the word petrified.

There was a pregnant woman just outside my door, about to give birth. I helped her. I held her bloody baby boy in my arms. The new mother reached up behind her, took an old shirt from her pack, wrapped the baby in it and got up and walked away. I asked her to come in to my apartment. She refused. (Years later, each time I went to the hospital to give birth, I reminded myself that, at least, I wasn't going to have to get up and walk away afterwards.)

A day or so later, I walked around the neighborhood to see what had happened. I passed a makeshift morgue a couple of blocks away from my apartment. There were corpses heaped up there—some headless, some missing arms or legs. There were guts everywhere. They just dug a big hole and pushed them all in. It was the first time I was scared.

The beginning of the new year usually was a very special time, filled with family gatherings. It was always a happy time. But 1968 isn't a year we want to remember, yet we can't forget it either. It changed so many people's lives. I faced the fear and felt a pain that had never existed before. I have never felt that way again—except 33 years later in my second homeland, when the twin towers of the Trade Center were destroyed on September 11, 2001.

This is a special New Year's dish. When the kids were growing up, I usually made a big batch on the weekend. We had it for brunch, lunch and breakfast the next day or for a snack in between.

Prepare the basic sweet rice and set it aside.
  2 egg crepes, shredded, set aside
  2 Chinese sausages, sliced thin
  ¼ c. dried shrimp, soaked in ¼ c. hot water for ½ hour
  ¼ c. minced shallot
  2-3 T. Golden Mountain sauce or soy sauce

In medium skillet, with 2 T. corn or soy bean oil, sauté shallots until fragrant. Add sausage. Cook approximately 2 minutes. Stir in shrimp. Cook extra two minutes. Turn off heat.

To assemble:

In a large deep plate, toss cooked rice with soy sauce. Arrange the egg crepe like a ring around the edge. Pour in sausage and shrimp. Sprinkle with freshly ground black pepper and crispy shallot, if desired. Serve warm or at room temperature.

The Egg Came First

THE AMERICAN PRESENCE IN VIETNAM CREATED MANY JOBS—BOTH LEGAL and illegal. One day, as I stood in line, waiting to check out at the gate of Bien Hoa Air Base, a military policeman approached a woman right in front of me.

"Ma'am, you have to come inside," he said.

"What for?" she said. "I haven't done anything."

"I believe we have to search your pants," he said.

"I will not," she said. "I haven't done anything wrong."

I looked down. A broken egg slid out of her pant leg. She couldn't see it, because it hit the tar behind her. As I watched, a second egg slid out of her pants. Both eggs sizzled on the hot tar. They weren't exactly over easy, but they weren't quite scrambled either.

She had seven cartons of cigarettes taped to her legs, and one dozen chicken eggs.

The two eggs that got away told her secrets.

Chicken Meets Egg Omelet

One:
  1 T. oil or butter
  ½ c diced bell pepper
  ½ c. diced sweet onion

Two:
  1 c. left over cooked chicken
  1 tsp. coconut powder
  1 tsp. yellow curry powder

Mix:
  4 eggs
  salt and pepper
  ¼ c. scallion
  ¼ c. cilantro

In a non-stick medium pan, sauté group 1 for 2-3 minutes. Add group 2. Toss around so the meat and vegetables have a good chance to get acquainted. Remove all to a bowl.

Back to the pan, add some extra oil or butter or cooking spray. Pour in egg mixture. Loosen around the edge so egg almost sets, then scatter chicken and vegetable mixture all around.

Then fold the cooked egg in half over the top of the mixture (so it looks like an omelet).

Tip: You may finish the omelet off in the microwave. Cook for a minute. Remember, don't put a metal pan or dish in the microwave.

Option: You may serve this with peanut butter sauce. (See sauce section)

Fresh Summer Rolls with Lobster

SHE WAS A BEAUTIFUL WOMAN—HALF VIETNAMESE AND HALF French. SHE was very slender and tall, with light brown hair, which cascaded all the way to her waist. Her American boyfriend hired me to cater a luncheon for her birthday.

We were at the bar inside his barracks, surrounded with food and drink. She was kissing him when a Vietnamese air force officer with a pistol in his hand and fire in his eyes, stormed in. Her husband.

It was at least 100 degrees outside, but I still felt a chill run through my spine. Unfortunately, it wasn't an uncommon situation at that time and place. Married women had affairs with American soldiers, mostly because of the money. Some actually fell in love. My friend had.

She didn't dare leave her husband for fear he would kill her. It appeared she hadn't been wrong in her fears.

From the moment he appeared at the door, I couldn't keep my eyes off his gun. Then, I spotted his finger move. Out of impulse, I picked up the vegetable platter and threw it right at him. Then I heard the gun shot. The bullet went through the ceiling. Everything happened so quickly. They pinned him down and called the MPs.

My friend's marriage, needless to say, didn't survive. He made her life a living hell before he ended the marriage—he got the car, the house, everything. She got nothing, even though she was the one who had made the money. The American boyfriend returned to the States. He never came back to marry her, as he had promised.

Oh, and the day's menu? Fresh summer rolls with prawns. How will I ever forget?

Fresh Summer Rolls with Lobster

THIS IS ONE OF THE DISHES VIETNAMESE CUISINE IS FAMOUS FOR. It is great for parties, because you can lay out all the fresh herbs, wrappers, sauce, cooked shrimp and meat and let the guests roll their own.

For each guest, you'll need:
  2 cooked lobster tails, shredded or 8 oz. cooked shrimp
  8 oz. cooked pork loin, sliced thin
  1 head Boston lettuce
  handful of fresh mint
  handful of fresh cilantro
  handful of fresh Thai basil
  1 c. cooked rice sticks (noodles)
  rice wrappers
  peanut butter dipping sauce (see the sauce section)

To assemble the rolls, dip rice wrapper into warm water. Lay the wrapper on a plate. First lay 1 piece of lettuce, then some rice sticks, then herbs, a piece of shrimp, a piece of meat. Roll up tightly. Then dip into the sauce.

If you serve as an appetizer, you only need 2 rolls for each guest. Then move on to the next course. This recipe will serve four as a first course.

To cook rice sticks: You don't need to soak the noodles, just drop the rice sticks in boiling water. When the water starts to boil again, set the timer for 4-5 minutes. Drain. Run cold water through to take the starch off.

The noodle texture should be soft and slightly crunchy, not mushy. Don't over cook.

Sweet Rice with Yucca Root

IN THE EARLY '70S, WORK WAS ALREADY SLOWING DOWN AT BIEN HOA. MY friend Dam and I came up with a scheme to make some money. Dam's boyfriend ran the little town down the road. There was a lottery system in Vietnam, like the Lotto here. People bought tickets. The numbers were read out over the radio. Dam's boyfriend suggested that Dam and I have our own lottery. So, we made our own rules. After all, how many times do people actually win anything? We'd split the proceeds three ways. Anyway, it sounded like a good idea. Dam's boyfriend owned a yucca farm, so the day of the drawing, we were sitting around, eating yucca root, when the number was read out—046. I choked on the yucca. Dam and I ended up paying out big money. I learned another important lesson that day—spread the risk.

You'd think I would have learned my lesson about gambling, but, no. After I came to the U.S., I was living in California, making $3.75 an hour. I had heard about Las Vegas from that Elvis movie, *Viva Las Vegas*. Some friends and I decided to go. I took $400—I lost it all playing black jack. I couldn't even afford a soda afterwards.

This is a simple, yet delicious dish.

Select 1 lb. of yucca, without any mold or cracks

Slit and peel off the bark-like skin

Cut into a short version of finger size and steam for approximately 20 minutes

Set aside

While the yucca is steaming, prepare the basic sweet rice, plus 1 tsp. salt. Half way through the cooking process, stir in cooked yucca. You may add an extra minute to the cooking time. Sprinkle with ¼ c. crispy shallot and enjoy!

Hot and Sour Shrimp with Sweet Pineapple Soup

THE AROMA OF THIS SOUP CAN EASILY TAKE ME ALL THE WAY BACK TO BIEN Hoa, where I learned how to make it for the first time.

The lady who cooked for the club, where I got my first job, taught and showed me a great deal about Southern Vietnamese food. For a newcomer from the north, I fell in love all over again.

She was responsible for the best Hot and Sour Eel and Banana Blossom Soup I ever ate. I didn't even know such a soup existed. Then she teamed it up with an amazing dish made from fried dried fish, which was then drenched in a hot, sweet and salty sauce. Right up my alley. Just thinking about it, gives me a head rush. Often, I know I like food just a little more than I should.

In the following recipe, I have simplified the process without sacrificing quality or flavor.

Hot and Sour Shrimp with Sweet Pineapple Soup

1 lb. large shrimp, peeled and de-veined, butterfly cut
2 tsp. salt*
2 tsp. sugar
1-3 tsp. hot pepper flakes
2 T. ground cumin
½ tsp. black pepper
In medium bowl, mix shrimp with the above seasonings.

8-10 c. broth
¼ c. fish sauce (No Substitutes)
1-2 tsp. concentrated tamarind juice (or white vinegar)
1 golden pineapple, cut in thin strips (approximately 5 cups)
2 c. cut up tomatoes, or one 15 oz. can whole tomatoes
1 bell pepper, cut into strips

In a medium soup pan, with approximately 2 T. oil, sauté shrimp for about 2

Hot and Sour Shrimp with Sweet Pineapple Soup

Beef with Rice Noodle and Basil, page 73

minutes. Remove from pan. Set aside.

Add 1 T. oil to the pan. Sauté the pineapple until it wilts (approximately 2 minutes). Pour in broth. You may use the mixture of broth and clam juice here. If you are using water, add a bouillon cube. Taste it carefully before seasoning further with fish sauce. Add tomatoes and peppers and bring to a boil. Depending on the tartness of the tomatoes, use your own judgment before adding tamarind or vinegar. When everything has come to a full boil, return shrimp to the pan. Stir and remove from heat.

If you are fortunate enough to have French mint, use it here (3 T. is sufficient). Add scallion and freshly sliced hot pepper.

*This isn't a misprint. What I am doing is creating a dimension for the shrimp of its own. You'll know why when you eat this soup. See if I'm right.

Lily's Essence

Lily was one of my good friends at Bien Hoa. We had met at a big party at the officers' club. We clicked immediately. Good food and great friendships have one thing in common—chemistry. She was smart and ambitious. I like those qualities in a person, male or female. She was responsible for turning a Regular Joe like me into a wheeling dealing entrepreneur. She knew everyone— military personnel on base, outside civilians in power, undercover cops.

Whenever I ran into her at parties, she was always with someone on the Who's Who list of important people in that town. One time, at an officers' club party, her date was a high ranking air force officer. Across the table from us was the flamboyant Nguyen Cao Ky himself, our vice president. Talk about an historic moment!

Around that time, soldiers were being pulled out of Vietnam. There were fewer jobs at the air base. The curfew became earlier and earlier. The night clubs and dance clubs were all closed. So Lily and I decided to open an underground café and dance club.

We were infatuated with the pilots (like my daughters are over Tom Cruise in *Top Gun*). We rented a big house and paid off the police. Our last night in business, we were dancing to "The Blue Danube," when we heard a lot of noise, footsteps outside, then the front door burst open. Police flooded in. Lily and I looked at each other. We knew right away these cops had to be from another town because we had already paid off the locals.

We were in business roughly a month and half before the bribes put us out of business. Cops from other towns wanted a piece of the action. We couldn't make enough money to pay everybody off. The pilots didn't really miss the dance club, but they did miss my food. I made lots of friends among the pilots. We let the good looking ones in for free. Maybe that's the reason we didn't make any money.

Not long after that, Lily moved back to Saigon, and I didn't hear from her for quite some time. Then, one day, there was a knock at the door. It was Lily, and she was in a rush. She said she needed money. I offered to take her to the bank. She said she didn't have time. She asked if I had any jewelry. Without any questions, I took off my 24-karat heavy gold chain with a good sized diamond stud and handed it to her. She gave me a quick hug, got back into the military jeep waiting for her outside, and I never saw her again. The necklace was mailed to me months later, with no return address.

The Lily I knew was never fond of cooking, but on rare occasions, she would make this dish to share with me. I believe it was the one dish she cared enough about to spend time in the kitchen. I treasure it, along with the echo of her laughter.

Lily's Essence

2 lbs. boneless pork butt sliced into thick ribbons, blotted dry with paper towels
¼ c. sliced shallot
3 T. brown sugar
¼ c. fish sauce or soy sauce
1/3 c. water
½ c. scallions, cut into ½ inch pieces
½ tsp. fresh ground black pepper
1 medium red bell pepper cut into thick strips
2 large sweet potatoes, cut into thick julienne

Arrange a single layer of sweet potatoes on a baking sheet. Bake until golden. Arrange on a serving plate.

In a hot wok, over high heat, drizzle 2 T. oil. Let the oil smoke before adding meat and shallots. Sear pork in 2 or 3 batches. This step will prevent pork from getting watery. (If it gets runny, you lose the aroma.) When the last batch is brown, remove it from the wok and set aside. To the wok, add the sugar. Let it carmelize. When the color changes from light brown to mahogany, return the pork to the wok. Stir well for 1 minute. Add cut up pepper, then add sauce and water. Cover wok. Cook for five minutes. Open wok. Stir in scallions and black pepper. Let sauce thicken for a minute or two. Pour over sweet potatoes. This will serve four.

Black-eyed Pea Pudding and Tapioca Coconut

As soon as we pulled out of the driveway, we knew we had a tail. This had to be the new guy. Someone on the inside had warned us. They had said he was new and hungry. Well, I wasn't new in this town, and I was most definitely not hungry, so I just had to play this guy for a fool, so he would know I wasn't an amateur at the game.

My operation wasn't a secret. Every cop in town knew about me. The only thing they didn't know was who I sold to. I wanted to keep that under wraps for more than one reason. Once I had made my delivery, it was up to the other party to take care of their own territory.

I told the driver to take Plan B. Depending on the destination of the drop, Plan A was to let the cop chase us for a while. We'd let him stop us and, of course, demand to inspect the vehicle. At that point, I'd reason with the guy and pay him off.

Plan B was to lead him to the highway where we could lose him. (Under cover cops wanting to make extra money on their own always ran solo and everyone of them seemed to drive an old Honda motorbike. We had a car, so, of course, we could run faster.)

Once on the highway, I knew several turns that could take us to an intersection. Even if he would be able to see which turn we made, he would still have to guess where we went from there. In most cases, if it was the cop's first time at giving chase, we would lose him.

He would do his homework and be back. Eventually, I would have to pay him off, but not this day. I made the drop, collected my money, and was back home in time for my afternoon snack, Black-eyed Pea Pudding with Coconut Tapioca.

I didn't ask for these adventures. They just sort of fell into my lap.

Black-eyed Pea Pudding and Tapioca Coconut

Some air force mechanics and pilots had approached me. Gasoline prices skyrocketed and it was next to impossible to find. These people were able to get gasoline directly from the fighter jets and they stored the stolen fuel in custom built false tanks in their vehicles. Each of these contacts had their own delivery schedules.

My black market career expanded. I lived in an apartment that had a fake wall, into which you could drive a small truck after all the display furniture had been pushed aside. My deliverymen would let me know they had a shipment for me. I'd clear the room. They would deliver the goods, and I would make sure the distributors were there to pick everything up. If buyers weren't there to pick up the goods immediately, I had the merchandise moved to a different location for storage.

I dealt with more than gasoline. Everything made in America was good, from chewing gum, to Ritz Crackers, to bar soap, to toilet paper, to canned ham. I also dealt in pricey stuff, like diamonds, watches, jewelry, etc. Items that made a good profit, and sold quickly, were alcohol and tobacco products. I didn't drink and I didn't smoke, but I knew all the best brands.

I learned very quickly and got very good at the job. I learned to get on good terms with the local undercover cops, paid them off to look the other way. Things didn't always go smoothly, but I usually managed.

For example, one time my supplier delivered a load of white sheets without telling me he was coming. I found out the police were going to raid, so I went to the building manager, a woman called Le, whose name meant "Fast."

She was a short woman, about as wide as she was tall. She had three or four kids, and she lived with those kids in a one-room building in the back. Her husband was a soldier. She got no paycheck, just a place to live. I still remember the look on her face the first time I rewarded her for her help. After that, whenever I needed her, she was always ready to help and she got even faster.

I told her about my problem with the sheets. The police showed up and searched and there was nothing to be found. Le had taken care of all the evidence in less than a half hour. That's when I found out that Le was her nickname. I can't remember her real name, but she definitely was "Fast."

Black-eyed Pea Pudding with Coconut Tapioca

2 T. small pearl tapioca
¾ c. water
½ tsp. salt
1 14-oz. can coconut cream

Bring to a boil. Simmer for 2 to 3 minutes. Add one 14 oz. can of coconut. Stir well. Set aside.

In a medium sauce pan, heat up two cups of water. Add ½ c. sweet rice. Bring to a boil. Cover. Simmer for about 20 minutes, stirring occasionally. While rice is cooking, drain a large can of black-eyed peas, about 3 ½ cups. Drain and rinse well. When the rice is cooked, add the peas and one cup of sugar to the rice mixture. Stir well. Cook an additional five minutes. Add one teaspoon of vanilla. Cover. Rest for 10 minutes.

To serve: Spoon ½ c. pudding into a dessert bowl. Top with ¼ c. coconut tapioca. Serve warm.

The Legend of Rum and Coke

ALL THE GIRLS AT THE CLUB KNEW HIM. HE WAS YOUNG, GOOD LOOKING and extremely generous with his tips. They called him the Rum and Coke guy. The drink at that time cost 25 cents, but his tip was always a brand new 500 *piesters*. (That would feed a family of four for at least 10 days.)

For weeks he was fair, giving every girl who worked there a chance to serve his drinks. Then one night, he only wanted one girl to wait on him. After that, he was no longer everybody's favorite customer. By then the twenty plus girls assumed his one and only waitress wanted him for one reason—his money.

Nothing could be further from the truth. The base rules were very strict. If a Vietnamese employee was caught outside the workplace, she could be arrested and lose her job. So, all she could do was to go in early so that might have lunch with him beside the club's garden.

Lunch became dinner one Sunday afternoon when he suggested that she call in sick and instead of going to work, she would visit him at his work place. She was very nervous about this, but the way she felt for him was more than enough to risk breaking the law. So he picked her up by the gate in his supply truck. They drove across the base to their rendezvous.

That afternoon, under a luminous light inside a warm supply room, she discovered what it was like to make love to a white man. The only other experience she had had was with her Vietnamese boyfriend, whom she had been dating for only a short time before meeting Rum and Coke.

After that afternoon, she tried to break up with her Vietnamese boyfriend, but he wouldn't have it. He knew the other man was an American. The Vietnamese boyfriend was the lead singer in a band. Everybody knew him, his face, his name. He easily could have had any woman he wanted. Only his pride was hurt. How dare she, a nobody, give him the brush off.

Before he walked out the door, he made sure she understood one thing: If she paraded around the base with any man, he would kill him. He kept his word, stalking her. If he wasn't around, he had spies, eager to score favor with him. They made sure she couldn't enter the base on her day off. Her life outside the base didn't mean anything to her after that.

All she could do was to think of Rum and Coke inside that gate and hold her breath until it was time to go to work, because that was the only place they could be together. In that noisy club and amid people, she only saw him, shining wherever he sat.

Sometimes his lips brushed hers in the club's hall, when no one was around. It was just as thrilling as the long and passionate one they had every night when she had to leave the club. She turned away from him with as much difficulty as a starving child would turn away from a plate of food.

Never before had she encountered such pain or such great desire for someone, the way she wanted him. She didn't tell him that it was only for his safety that they could only see each other at the club. Then, his time in Vietnam at an end, he had to go home.

On his last day, she managed to get inside his barracks and to stay with him one last night. That was only the second intimate time they had together. She had never known what it was to give someone her body and soul until that night. She worshipped every finger he laid on her. There was no tomorrow. Everything would end that night.

She noticed the half empty bottle of Pub while he was packing. She asked if she could keep it. That scent would forever remind her of their last night together.

She closed her eyes, weeping. Insanely, she thought, "If only I can slip into a coma right now, then I don't have to face tomorrow."

Of course, the next day came any way. At the terminal, the green suit she wore stood out like a tree among the gray swamp of G.I. uniforms.

There were no other females in sight. They kissed for the last time, long and salty. She looked up and saw tears streaming down from under his aviation sunglasses. With her handkerchief, she gently wiped them away, then cleaned her face. She told him she would put a curse into that piece of cloth, and he would never be able to forget her. He was confident that her curse would backfire. He brushed her cheek with the back of his hand, then he got in line. At the top of the stair, before he entered the military aircraft, he turned around as if to capture her last image.

The door closed behind him. The world tumbled down. Everything seemed to be in slow motion, as though time was out of control. "I'll never love anyone this way again," she vowed.

A Farewell Present for Sister Three

To honor the third born in the family, she was named "Number Three." She was the third in the family of twelve children, each having their own number. That afternoon when she failed to show up at our card game, I was suspicious. Some of us missed occasionally, but never Number Three.

At her apartment, the door was ajar. As I stuck my head in, I saw Sister Three curled up on the floor. I called out her name, but she didn't respond. Right away I noticed her clothing was soiled with a mixture of mud and blood. I rushed to her side and shook her shoulder. She slowly regained consciousness. I asked her what had happened.

When she told me, I felt a rage that I didn't even know I was capable of. I hailed a cyclo—a popular transport at that time, a bike with three wheels. The driver peddled in the back seat. The front was only big enough for two. Since it wasn't motorized, it didn't travel very fast, but it would still take a passenger from one point to another. Sister Three wasn't able to walk. We went straight to the police station. At the front door someone stopped us. I told them I would like to speak to the chief.

They told me I couldn't. At first I was very nice and calm. No one listened. The beast inside me came out. One hand on my hip, the other pounding the desk, I screamed, "Look at that woman! She just got raped by four men. As if that isn't enough, they beat her up and threatened if she came here to tell her story that they'll burn her parents' house down, and you say we have to stay in line and make an appointment?!"

The four men were arrested by the end of the day.

Such things don't just happen in war zones. Soon after I arrived in Los Angeles, I started networking for jobs. That's how I met Antonio, a young manager at a

Mexican restaurant near to where I was living at the time. He was impressed with my enthusiasm and promised to introduce me to a friend who owned an eatery across town.

He would pick me up the following Friday right after work and drive me to an interview he had set up for me. As soon as we passed the light, he turned toward a different direction. I asked where we were going. He said that he needed to stop at his apartment to change. I could wait in the car.

I sat in his car, which was parked only 20 feet from his front door. Soon he stuck his head out the door, with a phone to his ear.

"Hey! Come in. My friend has a question for you." He held the phone toward me.

This was a red flag for me. I hoped I was wrong. I filed my nails with a metal file as I walked toward the door.

"Oh, shoot! I just got disconnected. Why don't you sit down and get comfortable. I'll get him back. Maybe I'll just change my shirt, then we'll leave."

He left the door open and walked away. The couch was right beside the door.

"Okay," I thought. "Maybe I'm wrong. The door is open."

After a couple of minutes, he came back into the room without a shirt and with a drink in his hand. He offered it to me. I told him I didn't drink.

"You know, I went out of my way to get you a job. Maybe you should show me a little bit of appreciation."

"Sure," I said. "I'll buy you a bottle of tequila."

He started to laugh. No, he said, he didn't want tequila.

"You know, Antonio, I didn't tell you the whole truth. Not only am I under age, but I'm also a virgin. This isn't a good idea," I said gently.

I got up and walked out the door. As soon as I was outside, I turned around and looked right at him. My voice changed. "Today is your lucky day, because if you lay a hand on me, I'll make sure your ass will rot in a Los Angeles jail cell. Get your phone—if you even have one—and call a cab for me. Make sure you pay the cab or

I'll show up the first thing tomorrow at your restaurant and tell everybody you tried to rape me."

As I walked away, I should have felt my heart pounding, instead I had to fight the urge to throw myself on the ground and laugh out loud. *"I should have gotten an Oscar nomination for that performance,"* I thought to myself. *"Underage? A virgin? Where did that come from?"* The nail file had a blade on one side. I had planned that if I had to, I would drive it into his eyeball and then run for my life.

Sister Three and I lost track of one another. She got herself a different job and moved away from Bien Hoa. When we met again, I was delighted with her good news. She was engaged to marry a nice army sergeant from Oklahoma. He was already back in the States; her papers were in process. She was returning to Bien Hoa until she was ready to join him.

The years apart hadn't changed anything between us. We reconnected quickly. I sensed my friend was nervous about leaving Vietnam because she spoke little English and couldn't write any. I assured her that everything would be fine. She would be able to learn it along the way.

As a going away present, I gave Sister Three a playmate, a friend of my boss. I warned her about D.J. We hadn't nicknamed him Don Juan without a reason. I told her to have a great time—he would wine her and dine her and treat her like a princess. "But, whatever you do, don't fall for this guy," I warned.

She fell for him.

As the day to join her future husband drew nearer, she got edgier. Finally, she announced, "I can't go through with this. I'm not leaving." I felt guilty. I had created the situation with D.J. I decided I needed to solve the problem. After all, I had created it.

I told her I'd join her in the States. I'd get a temporary two-month visa. If I liked the States, I'd find a way to stay. I'd go back to Vietnam after she settled in. I needed an American fiancée to do this. Don Juan volunteered. He'd always teased me, but I told him I didn't have the stomach to fool around with a playboy. He asked how my stomach would do married to a playboy.

My visa wasn't ready by the time Sister Three left. D.J. went soon after she did. I was supposed to follow as soon as my paperwork was complete. I didn't. I never threw out that visa. I don't know why.

Chapter Four

LEAVING

Destiny

I<small>F IT WEREN'T FOR A FATEFUL DAY OUTSIDE</small> B<small>IEN</small> H<small>OA</small> C<small>ITY, ON THE</small> occasion of a gasoline delivery for the black market I operated, perhaps I would still be in Vietnam.

It was hot, humid. I remember I didn't feel very well, so I told the driver to stop the car because I needed to get out for a few minutes. That was when I saw the military truck approaching us. Naturally, my eyes followed it. To my horror, I saw that the back of the truck was filled with bloody body parts. First, I thought my eyes were playing tricks on me. But the driver confirmed my doubt. "Did you see what was in the back of that truck?" I couldn't answer him because when the stench hit the air surrounding me, everything in my stomach worked its way out. My head was spinning. "Is this 1968 all over again?" I asked myself.

Only a little over a week later, Saigon collapsed.

Later that same day, as soon as I was back at Bien Hoa, I paid a visit to a friend who worked in the intelligence department. I begged him to tell me what he knew. The look on his face haunted me for a long time. He just stared at me and said nothing for a while, then with a serious voice, he gave me advice I wasn't ready to hear—"If you can get out of the country, do it now. We're going down."

I was stunned. How could we all be living in the dark and not know any of this was happening?

I tossed and turned all night, wracking my brain, trying to think of a way to get out of Vietnam.

The only thing I had was an expired visa I had gotten two years previously when my boss had gone back to the U.S. He and his friend had worked out a plan so I could come visit them in the United States. I didn't go then, but I still had all the papers. That was my one and only hope.

As early as I could the next morning, I went to the U.S. Embassy in Saigon. I had no clue what I was going to do, but I just followed my gut instinct. I had to do something, anything but sit still and wait for the worst scenario.

I got another shock when I got to the Embassy. It was closed. There was a pool of people there, probably as panicked as I. We ended up talking to each other, speculating about what was going on. Just as I was about to leave, a man approached me. I had seen him standing beside a limousine earlier. He hadn't said anything. Now he said, "this Embassy is closed for good. They've set up a temporary one inside *Tan Son Nhat* Airport." To get there I would need his help. He could sneak me in—for a price. I agreed to pay. Luck was on my side because the money I had collected from the black market gasoline driver the day before was still in my purse. I had completely forgotten about it until that moment.

The man didn't appear to be surprised at my grabbing at his proposal, or that I had that kind of money on me. So, I got into the back of the limo, and we headed for *Tan Son Nhat* Airport.

When we were about to enter the main gate, he advised me to lay down and be very still. The police guard came and looked at the ID card from my temporary chauffeur. From the short conversation between the two men, I found out my driver worked for the Embassy. The police didn't bother to look at the back seat.

I felt flushed. Sweat started to trickle down my forehead. The last thing I wanted right now was to end up in a jail cell—military or civilian. I can't remember how long it took from the gate to our destination, but it sure felt like eternity. Finally, the vehicle stopped. My hand wasn't steady when I handed the driver a roll of money. Before he took off, he reminded me to be careful when finding a ride. Funny. On the way out, I hadn't worried about it at all.

I found myself at a regular barracks with a gray steel door, just like the ones

I had seen so many times at Bien Hoa, but as soon as I entered the door, the inside was just one big room set up like an office. To my right, along the wall, were desks with papers on them. To my left were desks with people. At the first desk sat a Vietnamese girl. She couldn't have been any more than 22 or 23. Two Americans sat at the heavy desk. In the middle of the room were all kinds of American military men, American civilian men and some Vietnamese females. I felt a little better. I didn't want to be the only female in the room. I wanted to blend in, not to stick out.

First, I figured I had to find out what was going on, so I decided to follow one guy whose wife or girlfriend was tagging along with him. I saw he picked up a whole bunch of forms to fill out, then brought them over to the Vietnamese woman at the desk. She looked through the papers, then signed one page and handed the stack to the guy next to her. The guy looked through the whole stack, then passed it to the last guy at the table. All he did was stamp it! I walked back and forth. I must have looked lost, because I heard a voice ask me if there were anything he could do to help. I turned around and chose my answer carefully. "Well, I don't know what form to fill out. My fiancé is not here. I would be very grateful if you can help me out."

"Where is your fiancé?" he asked.

"He's back in the United States." It just popped out. I had no idea where the words came from. It was a good thing he didn't ask any more questions. He picked up some forms, took a quick look at them and handed them to me. He told me what to do, and then he was gone.

I filled out the paper as he had advised me. In the area where it asked about my fiancé, I filled in the name of my boss's friend, his address, etc.

When I finished, I went straight to the Vietnamese girl, handed her my papers and said in Vietnamese. "I need your help. My fiancé is back in the United States. I can't get in touch with him. You've got to help me to get out of here."

With a puzzled look on her face, she flipped through my three pieces of paper, plus the two-year-old expired visa and told me something I already knew. "You don't have anything. I can't help you. How did you get in here? Let's just say, even if I wanted to help you," she pointed to the next guy and continued, "he's the one going to review your paper. Plus there is no way the big boss is going to stamp this. Without the Embassy stamp, where do you think you're going?"

In the middle of me nagging, begging for her help, and her saying she couldn't, someone a few feet away interrupted. The two guys at the table turned around and got up. Without a trace of hesitation, I leapt over, grabbed the stamp, and slammed it onto the bottom of my paper, right behind that guy's back. Then I turned around and faced the Vietnamese girl. Her eyes were popping out and her mouth was wide open. With my hand trembling, I handed her my piece of stamped paper. I heard my voice crack when I spoke to her.

"You said you wanted to help me, remember? Here's the big boss's stamp."

She shook her head, then wrote some numbers on top of the Embassy stamp, put the paper back into my hand, then pointed to the guard by the door, and gestured that I go over to see him.

What choice did I have but to walk toward that guy? I really didn't know what to expect, but all he did was glance at me, hand me a pass-like paper, and say, "All the information about your flight to Guam is in here."

I couldn't believe my ears. Had he said I had a flight that afternoon to Guam? The Vietnamese girl didn't blow my cover. She had given me a ticket to get out of Vietnam.

It had been only an hour since I had walked through the front door. The last 30 seconds changed my life forever.

I only had a few hours left and lot to do. Before I ran out of there, I expressed my sincere gratitude to the Vietnamese. I thanked her for her help and her kindness, which I will never forget.

The pass I got gave me a legal right to get out of *Tan Son Nhat*. I went home to say goodbye to my family.

Baby Back Rib Nuggets with Pickled Mustard Greens

THIS WAS THE LAST MEAL MY MOTHER AND I HAD TOGETHER IN VIETNAM. No one else was around, just the two of us in the kitchen, like old times. I'll never forget that moment. I told her about the complex situation I was in and asked for advice. I told her, "I have a chance to leave Vietnam today. In less than three hours, to be exact, the plane will take off. What should I do?" Should I stay and face an uncertain future with the new government, or should I leave and go to a strange, far away country where I didn't have a clue what would happen?

I knew better, but for some reason I hoped she would tell me to stay. I saw my mother age right in front of my eyes. With tears running down her cheeks, her hands shaking violently, she reached over and held mine. She urged me to take a chance and leave. Looking back, I think she held up remarkably. As a mother now myself, I can only imagine what I would do if one of my children came to me and told me she was leaving and that there was a chance we'd never see each other again.

Baby Back Rib Nuggets with Pickled Mustard Greens

2 lbs. baby back ribs*
2 cups pickled mustard greens**
1 can (14 oz.) whole tomatoes
2 T. sugar
1-2 T. fish sauce (or soy sauce)
¼ c. thinly sliced shallot (or onion)
2 cups broth or water

In a wok with high heat, add a thin coat of oil. When the oil starts to smoke, sear ribs until brown. At this point, sprinkle ribs with sugar and cook until the sugar caramelizes. Take the ribs from the wok and set aside.

In a heavy Dutch oven, sauté the shallots with the pickled mustard greens. Add tomatoes, broth and fish sauce. Transfer meat from the wok to the pan. Bring to a boil. Cover pan, lower heat and simmer for 40 to 50 minutes. For the last 10 minutes, take the lid off the pan so the sauce can thicken.

The result is chunks of ribs that are lightly sweet and tart with the unique aroma only pickled mustard greens can deliver. Sprinkle the ribs with freshly ground black pepper and serve with plenty of jasmine rice.

This dish is part of Northern Vietnam's repertoire. It's our family favorite.

*Tip: Buy ribs and ask the butcher to cut into 1 ½ inch sections. Take home and cut each separate section into nuggets.

**Look for pickled mustard greens in specialty food stores, or see the recipe in the chapter on vegetables.

Guam

THAT AFTERNOON, HUNDREDS OF US PACKED INTO A HUGE MILITARY CARGO plane, which took off, leaving Saigon and Vietnam, like a memory, behind. We were on our way to Guam. All I had with me was a small bag, which contained one set of clean clothes, a handkerchief my sister gave me for good luck, a $50 bill, folded neatly, then safely inserted into the seam of my shirt.

There was no time to feel anything. I was in shock.

I can't remember the flight from Saigon to Guam. I can't recall how I felt or what I did for the whole flight. It was late night—2 or 3 a.m.—when we landed in Guam, and as soon as I walked out of that plane, I was scared. The area between the plane and where they wanted us to go was full of secret service personnel (at least, that is what I thought they were, because beneath their open trench coats, I could see that they were fully armed).

Under the yellowish light, they stared at everyone who got out of the plane. I thought, "Oh, my God, any minute now someone is going to find out that I have no legal papers, and they'll send me right back to Vietnam." I was shaking. They took us to the mess hall where they served us pea soup and crackers before they moved us to our destination for the rest of the night.

Country Ribs with Pea and Vegetables Soup

THE FIRST CUP OF PEA SOUP I EVER HAD WAS IN APRIL 1975, EXACTLY one week before the fall of Saigon. I was lucky to get of *Tan Son Nhat* airport in the afternoon and landed in Guam around 3 a.m. That was where I had my first cup of pea soup. It was also my first meal away from Vietnam. A cup of that hot soup, filled with the kindness of strangers, is something I shall never forget. In less than 24 hours, I lost everything. I was alone, and there was no turning back.

Country Ribs with Pea and Vegetables Soup

2 lbs. bone in country pork ribs

Mix and coat the ribs with the following:
2 t. ground coriander seed
½ cayenne pepper
1 T. salt
1 T. sugar

1 c. chopped onion
1 c. chopped celery
1 c. chopped carrot
½ c. red bell pepper

16 c. water
1 lb. green or yellow dried peas, sorted, rinsed
2 chicken bouillon cubes
1-2 T. fish sauce*

Put the 16 c. water in a large soup pan. Bring water to a boil. At the same time, in a large, heavy skillet, brown the pork with 2 T. oil. Transfer meat to boiling water, together with the vegetables, seasoning and peas. Simmer for two hours. Remove bones from the ribs. Cut the pork into bite size. Return rib to soup. Adjust taste if necessary.

Sprinkle with cilantro leaves and chopped hot peppers, if desired.

*This depends on how salty the brand of soy or fish sauce is.

Crispy Fish with Lime and Chili Sauce

I NEVER GOT TO EAT THE STEAMED FISH FROM THE MESS HALL THAT afternoon in Guam. If I had done so, perhaps I would still be living in Guam. All my life, I never thought I would be so grateful to have missed a meal. Lime, chilies and crispy shallots create an intoxicating aroma. This dish is simple to prepare and incredibly delicious.

Mix well:
1-1 ½ lb. white fish, whole or fillets
salt and freshly ground pepper to taste
shallot oil

Lime Chili Sauce:
Juice of one lime
2 T. fish sauce
2-5 hot peppers, such as Birds Eye, Thai Dragon or Serano
1 T. sugar

Slice 2 medium cucumbers into ¼ inch rounds. Lay across a deep plate.

In a nonstick skillet, add 2-3 T. canola oil. Fry fish until it is crispy. Remove fish. Put it on top of cucumber slices. Pour lime sauce over. Sprinkle with 2 T. Crispy Shallots. Serve at once. Garnish with cilantro, if desired.

San Francisco

I DON'T KNOW WHAT I EXPECTED, BUT WHEN I WALKED INTO THAT HUGE building with a cement floor, crammed with people, I sank into a deep depression. All of those people had someplace to go, I thought. I could have kicked myself. Here I was, no money, no friends, in a building full of strangers, and all I could think about was the warm bed and my family behind me, in Saigon. They seemed so far away.

Hours later, I found myself sitting by the ocean shore, looking out over the sea and watching the sun come up on a new day. The young military policeman came back to check on me again. I think he worried about the young woman, sitting alone and staring out to nowhere for hours. He said I should go get some breakfast at the mess hall. He drove away, only to come back hours later to tell me I should get up. He gave me a can of soda and advised me to go eat lunch. They were cooking fish that day.

I guess it was time to get up, because I couldn't feel my butt any more. Or, maybe the word, fish, caught my attention. As I walked along side the shore, not particularly caring where I was going, I saw a building with a line of people waiting. I decided to check out what the line was for, before I headed on to the mess hall.

As soon as I walked through that door, I realized what was going on. My face burned hot and my chest pounded. I faced a scene identical to that at *Tan Son Nhat* Airbase. The Embassy paper work was being done right here. The only difference was that instead of the one Vietnamese worker in the front, they had two Vietnamese workers here. They looked like a brother-sister team. I worked out a quick plan in my head, but first, I had to go around and read all the forms to see if any there would benefit me. It was a futile hope. There was nothing for me.

Until this day, I still can't explain why I did what I did that particular day. I heard an inner voice speaking to me. Maybe I should call it a sixth sense, or intuition. Anyway, that voice urged me to do something and to do it quick. There was no time to think, so I did a re-enactment of the previous day. I went straight to the Vietnamese people, laid down my one piece of paper. With one breath I told them what had happened. I wrapped up my little speech by saying, "Yes, it looks bad. I don't have any excuse other than the desire to escape, to seek freedom." I added that I hoped they would help me get out of Guam.

As I had predicted, they were brother and sister. Both asked at the same time, in Vietnamese, "Where do you want to go?" Instead of giving them an answer, I asked a question: "Where are all these people going?" They told me, "The United States." "That's where I want to go," I said. "But you don't have any place to go," they argued. "I'll worry about that when the time comes," I said. "Right now, I want to get out of here."

They both spoke now.

"Listen, luck was on your side yesterday. Today is a different story."

"To get out of here, you have to have a marriage certificate, plus your husband has to be right by your side in front of the big boss."

"He's the one who will grant you permission to leave."

"We have no authority other than to write down your alien registration number."

"Why can't you give it to me?" I asked.

"What good will that do you?" one asked. "Need I remind you that you have got nothing here to work with, a big fat zero."

Then a miracle happened right in front of us. We heard noises. People were screaming. There was blood everywhere. A young woman was shielding her eyes with her hands. An older woman was viciously attacking her with the stiletto heel of a shoe, hitting her over and over. As I turned my head to watch, I noted right away that there was nobody at the table, except the two I was arguing with. They read my mind, because they both said it at the same time, "No! You wouldn't!"

I was incredibly calm. I walked over to the end of the table, quickly grabbed the Embassy stamp, then, just like the day before, stamped my paper. I raced back to my place in line, the ink of the stamp still wet on my paper.

They both stared at me, then at each other, then back to me, frozen with shock. "Yesterday *was* luck," I said. "Today I think is destiny. What do you think?"

Soon the place flooded with military police. They managed to handcuff the woman, who was cursing her husband nonstop. Evidently, the younger woman was her husband's secretary and mistress. The older woman had just figured it out when she caught her husband trying to sneak the younger woman out of the country.

My Vietnamese angels didn't blow the whistle on me. They granted me an alien registration number and helped me with the rest of the necessary papers. I walked outside, through the back door. There stood a humongous 747 with the door wide open, gleaming under the gorgeous sunshine.

I took a deep breath, waved goodbye to my almost one-day home, and walked inside that beautiful plane. Someone handed me a soft blanket as she took me to my seat. I fell asleep before the plane took off. When I opened my eyes, we were landing in Tokyo, Japan, to refuel. I fell asleep again. When I woke up the second time, I was informed we were about to land in the northern part San Francisco, California.

Chapter Five

A New Home

Chase Away the Blues Beef

I awoke to a chirping cry outside the window screen and the Northern San Francisco chill. We flew straight from Guam to a military base in a San Francisco suburb. Because it had been really late the night before, I roomed with an Air Force doctor, his wife and their children. They had evacuated from Saigon at the same time I did. We stayed in officer housing inside the base.

As I lay there that morning, my thoughts traveled to Vietnam: I wasn't in Saigon or Bien Hoa any more. I was in the United States of America. I'd made it. How cool, I thought. Then, after my elated feelings of victory, I was slammed down by reality. Where would I go from here? I didn't know a soul in this far away land. I had been told the night before that I might be released that morning. Where would I go?

The cry outside my window got a little louder. It drew me out of bed and I walked toward it. There, outside the window, on a branch was a little bird. She was wet, her tiny feet shaking. She seemed lost, just like me.

I thought I was holding up well, but at that moment I lost it. I wept and sobbed, and sobbed and wept. I told myself, "Oh, come on, get hold of yourself. You're tough. You can handle this and more." But, another voice inside was screaming, "Go ahead and cry. What else do you have to lose? You've lost everything. You're homeless. You have nobody, no family, no money."

As I was drowning in my own sorrow, I smelled a wonderful odor coming from the other room: the scent of home. There was the aroma of Vietnamese food that I had been missing for days. I said goodbye to my little friend and moved as fast as I could toward the kitchen. When I caught sight of what was on the table, I felt like I was Alice in Wonderland. To my delight, there was a big bowl of stir fry beef with vegetables and an even bigger bowl of rice. How this woman accomplished so much in such little time in a strange place was a lesson I learned when I had kids of my own. If you have kids, you'll find the way to feed them, no matter what.

Very cheerfully, she said she thought we all could use a decent meal with some real food. My voice cracked when I told her that I appreciated it more than she would ever know. With the food from home, I didn't feel sad any longer. I was ready and set for my journey. After the meal, we said goodbye and went our own ways. I wished later that I had asked her for her address so I could have sent her and her family a thank you note.

As long as I live, I will never forget that meal or the kindness of strangers thrown into tough circumstances. There was power in Beef Stir Fry with Vegetables to heal. To that woman and her family, I now say thank you.

Chase Away the Blues Beef

8 oz. round, flank or shell sirloin beef steak, sliced thin
½ tsp. salt
½ tsp. sugar
¼ tsp. black pepper
1 tsp. vegetable oil
Mix well and set aside.
1 large onion cut in thick julienne fashion
6 cloves garlic (2 T. minced)
1 lb. string bean, washed, trimmed and cut in half
8 oz. mushroom sliced

Sauce:
Mix
1 T. fish sauce
1 T. light soy sauce
1 T. oyster sauce
1 tsp. sugar
1 c. broth or water

In a smoking hot wok, add 2 T. oil, then beef. Sauté for 1-2 minutes. Remove beef from wok. With 1 T. oil, sauté onion 1 minute. Add garlic. Cook 1 more minute. Toss in vegetables. Keep stirring. Pour in sauce. Mix well, then cover wok. Cook for 8 minutes. Take off the lid. Add beef. Cook until it is heated through, 1-2 minutes.

Like all fast cooking dishes, this is best served right away.

Tip: When putting the beef back into the wok, don't put the cover back on. The string beans will lose their green color.

Blue Sea

IT'S FUNNY HOW FOOD MAKES YOU THINK OF PEOPLE (AND VICE versa). MY mother had a thing for blue, so each of her daughters was named Bich (blue) something. The sister third in line was Bich Hai (Blue Sea). She was a stunning girl, with dark hair and long legs. She was the only girl in the family to get into the most prestigious public school in Saigon. (Only the top 10 smartest girls in the country could pass through its gate.)

She was always studying. Every time I came home, most likely I would find Bich Hai sitting by her desk with a stack of books and a big bowl of boiled or roasted peanuts. Sometimes I was actually able to get her away from that pile of books. We would ride into Saigon on her Honda mo-ped. We would go to movies, get ice cream, or go shopping—girl stuff.

I always enjoyed her company, even though she was my opposite. One time we were late. We were on our way to see *Dr. Zhivago*. She drove a little too fast around the rotary in front of the Saigon Market. We heard the whistle and the policeman pulled us over. I could see that Bich Hai was nervous. She said this had never happened to her before. (I was always a bad influence.)

The policeman was obnoxious. He was in her face, shouting. He was a jerk. As Bich Hai apologized, without saying a word, I reached into my purse, folded a 500 piasters bill neatly into the palm of my hand and held my hand out to the policeman as though I wanted to shake hands. I slipped the bill quickly into his hand. I watched as he glanced at the bill, made sure he got the amount he wanted, then signaled us to move along.

As soon as we moved away, my sister was furious with me. "What if he hadn't taken the bribe?" she asked. "What if he had put us in jail?"

How could I explain to my little sister, the one who would never break the rules, not even for all the peanuts in Georgia, that I did this kind of stuff all the time. She lived in a world different from mine. I dealt with a system that was so messed up there was no justice anywhere. Money would buy just about anything. A speeding ticket was nothing.

We finally made it to *Dr. Zhivago*. We wept, watching Lara leave her handsome doctor. When the camera came in close to show his eyes, we could see his pain and sorrow. It was heart breaking. We cheered ourselves that beautiful day with mango ice cream and a pile of chantilly on top.

When I left Vietnam, Bich Hai gave me a handkerchief and a necklace for good luck. I still have them with me. We kept in touch. She wrote to me regularly, just to let me know what was going on at home. In one letter she told me about her dream of wanting to live peacefully in a small house with a white picket fence and red roses in the garden.

A couple of months went by. There were no letters from Bich Hai. I worried. Then I had a dream. In it, I stood inside a tunnel with a white cloud around me. I saw Bich Hai right in front of me. I reached for her, but I couldn't touch her. She wore a long white dress, which was drenched with blood. Her head was bleeding. I heard myself screaming as she drifted away in that white smoke. I opened my eyes. I was sitting upright in bed, screaming. I wrote my mother immediately and insisted she tell me what had happened. Why hadn't Bich Hai written?

My mother's letter brought no good news. Bich Hai had been on her Honda mo-ped when someone yanked at her pocket book, which she had draped across the front of her body. He pulled so hard that he pulled her off her bike. Her head hit the pavement. She was already brain dead when my mother arrived. Someone had killed my sister the day before my dream. Whenever I make anything with peanuts, I think of my sister, Bich Hai.

Roasted Peanuts

2 lbs. raw peanuts, shelled. (Approximately 3 cups)

Preheat the oven to 350 F. Make sure the rack is in the middle of the oven. Spread the peanuts in a single layer in a heavy jelly roll type pan. Roast until the color turns golden, not brown (18-20 minutes). From time to time, shuffle and rotate the pan. Watch it closely the last five minutes. Cool. Chop in a food processor until the peanuts are in small broken pieces. If you don't own a food processor, use a large plastic bag. Put the peanuts into the bag. Make sure you let the air out. Then, roll with a rolling pin.

Peanut Butter Dipping Sauce

¾ c. water
½ c. creamy peanut butter (store bought or home made)
3 T. brown sugar
3 T. soy sauce
½ tsp. salt
3 ½ T. rice or white vinegar
½ tsp . – 1 T. hot pepper flakes
1 T. crispy shallot
1 T. crispy garlic

In a blender, or medium-size bowl with hand blender, mix until well blended. Garnish with fresh chopped peanuts, sliced chilies, fresh mint and cilantro. This makes 1 ½ c. dipping sauce.

Use it for dipping vegetables, or as salad dressing, or on fresh rolls. Drizzle over rice noodles, fried rice, etc. I can go on and on, but it's your turn to experiment.

Grilled Pork in Green Salad with Herbs and Rice Noodles

IT'S HARD NOT TO THINK OF TINY SANG WHENEVER I MAKE THIS DISH. Her name was Sang. I don't know how she ever got the nickname Tiny, because by any stretch of the imagination, she wasn't tiny.

She took me in when I first arrived in Long Beach, California. I will always be thankful for her kindness. She sheltered me and helped me find a job at the Max Factor plant. Eventually, I was able to get myself a nice apartment right below her place. We had a lot of fun communicating with each through my ceiling and her floor.

One day there was more than one bang on top of my light, meaning she was coming down and would have some cool things to share with me.

When she came downstairs, however, she insisted that we go out to lunch to a new restaurant in town that not only made very good noodle salad, but we'd get to meet a big celebrity. She went on and on about how, if we were in Vietnam, we wouldn't be able to hang out with this guy. Finally, I asked her who the big shot was? As soon as she told me his name, there were butterflies in my stomach. I said to myself, "Tiny, you'll be the one to get the shock." We walked in amidst the lunch crowd, and there he was.

It was years later, and a world apart, but it was him. It wasn't a concert hall or Maxim's dance floor (where he used to perform), or me behind him, running around Saigon on his moped, but here we met again. He moved toward us, and we hugged. Out of the corner of my eye, I saw Tiny's eyes pop and her mouth drop open. I can't remember what he said to me, but I will never forget he told Tiny I was his old flame. We talked about the old times. Emotions ran high, not because once upon a time we had dated, but because we were sitting half a world away from all that had been familiar and loved. We'd both lost our home, our country, and that loss had shaped our lives and changed us forever.

Grilled Pork in Green Salad with Herbs and Rice Noodles

Fresh Summer Rolls with Lobster, page 100

Of course, Tiny always wanted to go back to that restaurant, because she liked a particular salad that they made. I volunteered to make it for her. She rolled her eyes. I shocked Tiny again. Between mouthfuls, she said we could open our own restaurant and give my old flame a run for his money. I joked with her, "Who will go shopping for clothes between trips to Las Vegas to play black jack for us if we open a restaurant?"

Actually, more than once, I wondered what would happen if I took her suggestion and pursued the food business. But, I was free and having a good time. One thing I know for sure, if I had gone into the restaurant business then, I would never have come to find Maine.

This is a great casual get together dish. Lay everything on the table. Guests will serve themselves. There are many happy memories behind this dish for our family, as well as the people I cater for.

Grilled Pork in Green Salad with Herbs and Rice Noodles

3 lbs. pork loin, tenderloin or boneless ribs. Cut into ribbons 2"x3", approximately ¼ inch thick
2 T. fish sauce
2 T. soy sauce
2 T. caramel
2 T. brown sugar
½ c. scallion, cut into ½ inch pieces
1 tsp. black pepper
1 tsp. ground coriander
1 T. shallot oil or vegetable oil
¼ c. water

In a large bowl, whisk marinade into a paste. Add pork. Mix well. Marinate pork from 2 hours to overnight.

1 lb. round rice noodles (Bun)
2-3 heads of Boston lettuce
1 bunch of mint
1 bunch of cilantro
2-3 cucumbers, peeled, cut into thin (or thick) slices, depending on your taste

Scallion oil (See the appendix, Sauces and Garnishes)
Coarsely chopped roasted peanuts
Salad dressing fish sauce (see the appendix)
Pickled carrots and daikon (see the appendix)

In a large pan, bring 4 quarts of water to boil. Drop in rice noodle. Stir constantly, until water boils again. Cook for five minutes. Drain and rinse well with cold water. Prepare vegetable platter. Situate everything on the table.

Either grill the pork directly on a barbeque rack, or thread it onto wooden or metal skewers. Grill 3-4 minutes per side.

To serve as a salad bowl:
In a large soup bowl, break up about ½ c. lettuce. Add ¼ c. cucumber with

cilantro, mint (as desired). The next layer will be approximately ¾ c. rice noodles, then the grilled meat will be on top with 1 T. chopped peanuts, 2 tsp. scallion oil and 3-4 T. dressing. Toss well and enjoy.

To assemble as a salad roll:
In each piece of lettuce, put in approximately 1 T. rice noodles, a couple of sprigs of herbs and shredded cucumber, 1 piece of meat, a touch of scallion oil, pinch of peanuts. Fold the lettuce over to form a roll, then dip into a small bowl of dressing. Serves 6-8.

An East Meets West Love Story

Once upon a time, a merchant marine from back East (a small Maine town called Corinna) ventured into the big city of Long Beach, California, out on the West Coast.

He walked into a club, not knowing his destiny would be tied to a barmaid who worked there. She noticed him because of his good looks. He started to pay attention to her after a couple of free drinks.

The next time his ship docked in Long Beach, she invited him to a home cooked meal. After he ate, he walked around her apartment and fixed everything that was broken. "Aha," she said to herself. "This guy is handy."

Twenty-five years later, she still cooks for him, and he still fixes everything that goes wrong around the house. Just like every married couple, they have their ups and downs. In fact, they have nicknames for one another. She lovingly calls him her PITA (and, no, she didn't name him after the flat bread). After all these years, she still remembers the first three-course meal she cooked for him: Stuffed Crab Shells, Baby Back Ribs with Pineapple, and Hot and Sour Soup. Talk about the power of food.

East Meets West Meat Loaf

1 large onion, chopped and caramelized with 1 tsp. sugar
1 ½ lb. lean ground beef (90 percent lean)
2 T. oyster sauce
1 T. soy sauce
1 T. granulated garlic
2 eggs
½ c. bread crumbs
1 tsp. cayenne pepper (optional)
½ tsp. black pepper

In a hot skillet with 2 tsp. vegetable oil, sauté the onion for 2-3 minutes. Add sugar. Stir constantly until onion is nicely brown (2-3 minutes). In a large bowl, mix onion and the rest of the ingredients. Shape into an oval loaf. Make a trench in the middle of the loaf for glaze.

In a small bowl, mix the glaze.
½ c. ketchup
2 T. brown sugar
2 tsp. chili and garlic sauce
1 T. Sriracha hot sauce (optional)

Pour glaze into the loaf trench. Bake in a 350 degree oven for 1 hour and 30 minutes. To serve, make sandwiches with pita.

Gloria's Chicken

MY MOTHER-IN-LAW GLORIA IS THE LADY WHO IS RESPONSIBLE FOR turning a city slicker like me into a serious gardener. It was July 1977 the first time I walked into her vegetable garden. My one and only reaction was, "There is something wrong here. Why would anyone want to go through this much work, just to have vegetables to eat?" I didn't say anything, but I was not impressed.

But, then came August, and I found myself excitedly picking the flawless beans off their bushes. September strolled by, and I marveled at the big beautiful red tomatoes hanging heavily over their cages. One day, she said, "The corn is ready," as she put a big pot of water on to boil, then dashed out into the garden. She came back with a bag full of corn ears, pulled off the husks, and dropped yellow corn into the boiling water.

I couldn't stop eating. I must have consumed somewhere between 12-15 ears of corn that afternoon. Normal people might have gotten sick, but I'm not normal.

I knew what my next project would be, but who knew it would take a lifetime to perfect? After all these years, I think I've done a bit with two vegetable gardens and eight flower beds.

Thank you, Mother, for passing on to me your labor of love for nature. You're still the best gardener I know. This is her favorite chicken dish.

Gloria's Chicken

1 4-5 lb. young whole chicken, skin removed

Cut off wing tips, then cut apart at the joints of the leg and thigh. Cut breast into 6 pieces. Set aside.

Spices:
  3-4 oz. julienne sliced ginger
  ¼ c. brown sugar

Sauces:
  ¼ c. soy sauce
  2 T. fish sauce
  ½ c. water

In a hot wok, with 2 T. canola oil, sauté the ginger. This step takes about 2-3 minutes. Next, add the brown sugar. Watch the sugar carefully. This is the crucial point of this dish. You are about to create a caramelized ginger flavor for the chicken process. When the sugar turns a nice glossy brown, add the chicken and keep stirring for the next 4-5 minutes. Pour in sauce. Bring to a boil. Cover, then lower heat to medium. Cook for 25-30 minutes, stirring occasionally. The last five minutes, take the lid off the pan so that the sauce can thicken a bit, but don't let it all vaporize. You should have about ½ of the sauce left. Sprinkle in freshly ground black pepper. Serve with your favorite steamed vegetables. The ones I generally serve with this dish are: cabbage, beet greens or baby bok choy. Last, but not least, make sure you have a big bowl of rice. Serves 4-6.

Monster Soup

IF THERE'S ANY SUCH THING AS KILLER LOOKS, MY LITTLE MONSTER HAS them. Amanda was a 10-pound baby, with dark hair so long that she had her first hair cut when she was barely four-days old.

She was born with an athletic gift; she believed she could do anything—as we told her—that a boy could do. The result was that she is a fearless dare devil. That's why I call her my Little Monster.

Another talent that Amanda has is the ability to consume a whole lot of food without ever putting on weight.

She went through college with ROTC, on a scholarship from the U.S. Navy. In May 2002, on one sunny afternoon, hers was the first name called at the commissioning ceremony. My heart skipped a few beats when I saw my daughter emerge from the U.S.S. Constitution in her impeccable white uniform. She walked with her head high and her face full of determination.

My emotions were on a rough roller coaster ride that day. I wept with joy when she got her first salute. I doubt anyone was more proud than I was at that moment. My daughter chose to serve her country, the place that took me in when I had no where else to go. Her decision to enter the military makes me feel as though I'm giving something back to this great country.

But, it was difficult that cloudy January 17, 2003, when I watched on television as her ship left San Diego for the Middle East. In my mind's eye, I see my Little Monster as the little girl she was. I have to remind myself that she is now a combat systems officer aboard the U.S.S. Dubuque, grown up, professional, and starting a new chapter in her life.

I still remember that fall day in 1998 when we checked Amanda into Boston University. One item we carried into her room, I can guarantee no one else had: a case of homemade soup, cooked and canned in jars, made from freshly harvested vegetables. It became a ritual every fall until she graduated.

Monster Soup

3 T. shallot sliced thin
2 T. minced garlic
2 c. fresh cut up tomatoes or 1 can (14.5 oz)
4 c. cut up fresh corn or 2 cans vacuum-packed corn
6 c. broth
1 bottle of clam juice (8 oz.)

Seasoning:
1 T. fish sauce
½ tsp. salt
1 T. white vinegar
1 tsp.-2 T. hot sauce (depending on taste)

Herbs:
1-5 Thai Dragon peppers, sliced thin
½ tsp. fresh ground black pepper
½ c. combination scallions and cilantro

In a medium-sized soup pot with 2 T. canola oil, sauté the shallots until lightly brown at the edges. Add garlic. Watch it very carefully because garlic can burn quickly. Add tomatoes and corn. Stir well so the vegetables have a chance to absorb the flavor of the shallots and garlic, then pour in broth and clam juice. Season with care, depending on how much sodium is in your broth and the brand of the fish sauce you're using. Bring soup to a boil. Remove from heat, toss in herbs, peppers and sliced chilies.

Normally serves 4-6. Amanda-sized serving, 1.

Note: If you don't like cilantro, use fresh dill instead.

Princess's Dessert

WE BOTH LOVE THE STORY "THE LITTLE PRINCESS" FROM FRANCES Hodgson Burnett, with the character named Sara Crewe. That story is how I started the nickname for my own Little Princess.

Of my three girls, Sara Maie is the most exotic looking, and she's the only one who has shown an interest in cooking. When she was in the play pen, all I had to do was throw in some plastic pots and pans, and she would entertain herself for hours. When she got a bit older, I was usually in the kitchen by the stoves. She would be very comfortable, sitting on top of my foot with her little arms wrapped around my leg.

"Mama cooking. Mama make good food," she would say.

Time has flown by, and she has turned into a beautiful young lady. More than once, she has said to me, "Someday, somebody important will discover your talent and you'll be famous." I told her I'm already famous now. I'm her mom.

Sara, like her older sister, went to college on a ROTC scholarship. One day in May 2004, I was the proudest mom in America, watching my second daughter get her first salute.

Thank you, Princess. I feel so blessed having you in my life.

Just like Sara, this dessert is sweet and exotic.

I use two cups of cooked beans in this recipe, but usually the dried mung bean comes in 14 oz. bags. You may use half the bag and freeze the rest for later use in Sweet Rice with Toasted Sesame and Coconut.

> **14 oz. bag dried mung bean, soaked over night.**
> **Steam over high heat for 20-30 minutes**
>
> **2 c. cooked mung bean, tossed with ¼ tsp. salt**
> **3 c. water**

1 c. sugar
3 T. tapioca starch, mixed with ¼ c. water
1 tsp. vanilla

Bring water and sugar to boil. Gently stir in tapioca. Mix. When the mixture thickens, which is usually in less than a minute, fold in beans and vanilla. Serve with (lightly) salted coconut cream.

1 can coconut cream (14 oz) mixed well with ½ tsp. salt.

To serve, ladle hot bean soup to medium-size bowl (2 parts bean to one part coconut). Add a dollop of coconut cream. This is a very popular dessert among my customers

Baby Love's Chicken

SAMANTHA MARIE IS MY "BABY LOVE." AMONG THE OTHER FOUR FAMILY members, Sammie has over 30 nicknames. Needless to say, we all adore her.

I marvel at the nature of genes. She was delivered Caesarian. Since the moment the doctor cut me open and pulled her out, she was totally a Caucasian baby, with dark blue eyes and light, light hair. She has grown into a long-legged American beauty, with the brains to match.

Just looking at her, you would never guess her favorite food groups are sugar and fat.

I can't imagine she will ever fix a dish of vegetables for herself. Lucky for her, I'm always home at meal times. I owe it to Sam to get to know all the latest noises in rap—I will not call it music—and teenager flicks.

In the winter, Sam's Sunday morning game is called "torture Mom time," which she is very fond of playing. She pins me down with her spider legs, and I have to tell her a string of boring stories while she pokes, chokes and tickles me. I enjoy the game. It lets me do a lot of screaming in terror.

We can't do this game in the summer, because we do a market together every Sunday in Bar Harbor, Maine. We laugh a lot to match the food we consume on the road. Soon she'll be graduating from high school and continuing her studies somewhere.Someday, when I'm six foot under or my ashes scattered all over the ocean somewhere, one thing is clear. Our laughter and the way she makes me feel will live on. Thank you "Baby Love." You're my proud treasure bonus.

This is Samantha's favorite chicken dish. Crispy pieces of chicken, laced in savory sauce, perfumed with wine, ginger and toasted sesame seed. All that, on top of a pile of crunchy, tender string beans. Sweet and spicy—just like Sam.

1 ½ - 2 lbs. boneless chicken breast, cut into cubes
3 T. water chestnut powder
2 T. mirin cooking wine
1 T. granulated garlic
2 T. light soy sauce
1 T. garlic oil
2 tsp. sesame oil

Mix well and set aside.

4-6 c. oil for deep frying
2 T. sesame seed
1 lb. string beans, washed, trimmed, dried well
2 T. grated ginger
2 T. ketchup
3 T. brown sugar

2 T. soy sauce
½ c. broth

In wok, with medium heat, toast sesame seeds until fragrant and lightly brown. Remove. Set aside. Turn heat up to high. Pour in oil. Heat oil to 350 degree. Deep fry beans for 2-3 minutes. Remove beans. Put on a few pieces of paper towel to blot out excess oil, then lay beans on serving plate.

Next, cook the chicken in the wok. Fry a few pieces at a time. Keep the temperature steady and have a stainless steel bowl nearby to empty hot oil into.

Remove cooked chicken to a large plate lined with paper towel. Chicken should be crispy, with a light brown color. Empty out oil, leaving behind approximately 1-2 T. oil. Add ginger to wok. After ginger releases aroma (1-2 minutes), add sugar and ketchup. Cook and stir constantly at this point. You want to work the brown sugar and ketchup to create a glaze. Pour in the broth and soy sauce. Bring the sauce to rapid boil for 1-2 minutes. Return the chicken to the wok. Toss it well to coat with the sauce. Sprinkle in toasted sesame. Serve chicken over crispy string bean and fried rice. Serves 4-6.

Claudia's String Beans

MY SISTER-IN-LAW CLAUDIA IS ITALIAN. ONE SUMMER DAY WHEN SHE visited, I made this dish with string beans I had just picked out of the garden. Claudia must have liked it, because the dish never made it to the table. I told her that I'd name the dish after her.

> 2 lbs. fresh young string beans, washed and trimmed
> 2 T. canola oil

Spice Paste:
> 2 T. minced lemongrass
> 1 T. minced garlic
> 1 hot pepper, such as Thai Dragon or 1 tsp. dried hot pepper, crushed

Mix the above ingredients together.

Sauce:
> 1 c. chicken broth
> 2 T. fish sauce
> 1 T. sugar
> ½ tsp. salt

In a hot wok, sauté the spice paste until fragrant. Add beans. Stir two to three minutes. Add sauce. Mix well. Cover. Cook until beans are tender crisp (six to eight minutes). Sprinkle with black pepper and serve as a side dish.

The King's Chicken

There are times when I accept big catering jobs and find myself surrounded by what resembles a mountain of all kinds of different dishes. Who would guess that this simple dish can reward me with so much pleasure? Once upon a time, I made this dish for our dear friend, Steve King, and his new (at the time) bride. Steve now rests in God's care. His death was a long, slow process, caused by a brain tumor. On his death bed, he told me, "You're still the only one I know that can take a chicken and make a party out of it." You bet!

We continued to talk, even after he had died. He would come to me in my dreams. Sometimes he would give me advice. Other times, he would bring me exotic fruits. Always, he was there with his kindness and charm, as he had been in life. One time, two days before Christmas, as I was overwhelmed with the stress of work and the holidays, he came to me in dreamland and said, "I've come to take you out to lunch!" We went to an open air café I used to visit in Saigon.

I knew it was a dream, but I couldn't help but marvel at the colors surrounding me. We ate. We laughed. I savored the moment. The last time I saw Steve in my dreams, was that following March. He was looking boyish and very happy. He was waving a piece of paper at me. "I came to say goodbye," he said. "I've got a red ticket."

I woke up and tearfully told my husband, "Steve is gone. I'll never see him again." And, I never have. But, I think of him every time I make his favorite chicken.

The King's Chicken

1 4-5 lb. whole chicken (free range, preferably)
3-4 lime kaffir leaves, or 1 large lime, peeled—reserve the juice
trim the white off the peel
cut the green into small strips
1 lb. Napa cabbage, shredded
1 medium carrot, julienne cut
3 small blocks bean vermicelli (4 oz.), soaked in warm water
1 tsp. salt
3 T. fish sauce (or soy sauce)
½ c. cut up scallion and cilantro

For dipping sauce:
Mix in a small bowl:
Juice from lime
2 T. crushed ginger
1 T. fresh minced garlic
2-5 freshly sliced hot peppers (optional)
2 T. brown sugar
1/3 c. fish sauce or soy sauce (approximately)—do this by taste

Wash chicken, rinse well, put in a large stock pot. Barely cover it with water and lime leaves (or peel). Bring to a roaring boil. Keep the heat at medium until chicken is cooked through. The cooked chicken should be at the firm stage—not falling off the bone. (This takes about 45 minutes or just a bit longer, depending on the stove's temperature.) Remove chicken. Let it rest for 10 minutes while the soup is cooking.

Skim off the fat from the broth, season with salt and fish sauce. You might need some extra help here with a bouillon cube. Remove the lime leaves/peel, and add the bean thread, Napa cabbages and carrot. Bring to a boil. Add scallion and cilantro. Sprinkle in ½ tsp. black pepper (freshly ground, of course).

To serve:
Slice, or cut, chicken into pieces. Arrange beautifully on a large plate. Each guest will have his or her own small bowl of dipping sauce, a medium bowl of rice and a large bowl of soup. Eat the soup with the rest of the meal. Dip a

piece of chicken in dipping sauce, put it on top of your rice, lace it with the vegetables from the soup—and enjoy.

Thank you Steve King. We will treasure forever the memories of your friendship.

EPILOGUE

The New Life

I FEEL BLESSED FOR WHERE I AM RIGHT NOW. I HAVE WISHED TO SHARE some of the things I've learned and have worked hard to perfect. I feel obligated to share some of the secrets of my lost Saigon with my children, and, at the same time, to pay tribute to my mother's lessons. They've given Saigon another name now, and maybe, in time, and with this celebration of old Saigon, I will be able to accept that as part of my healing process.

So here it is. Twenty-nine years later, almost half a life time away, I'm still cooking, blessed with many loyal customers.

May 22, 2004, inside beautiful Goddard Chapel at Tufts University, Sara Maie, my little princess, received her commission in the U.S. Navy. Amanda, Lt. J.G., flew in from San Diego, to attend. Sara was the only female in the Navy ROTC at Tufts. She was also the only female at the commissioning ceremony. She stood out like an exotic white orchid amidst the Army uniforms.

Her name was the last called. Her grandmother whispered, "They saved the best for last." "You bet," I whispered back.

That moment was frozen in time. I marveled at the sight of my two girls on stage. One looked like a swan, the other resembled an orchid. Amanda administered the oath to her sister. Her uncle Thomas and her aunt Susan revealed her rank, one on each side. Her father lovingly placed her Navy hat on her head. I joined them on stage. My princess was doing just fine until she caught my eye. We both teared up.

I am so proud of my children. They are my source of inspiration. I took a deep breath. Watch out world because Sara Maie is about to fly. She joins the crew of the U.S.S. Curts in San Diego. She and her sister will at least be based in the same town. Samantha will one day join her sisters. I can almost see it now. The all-American beauty with the mile-long legs in her white uniform. I get goose bumps just thinking of my three girls together.

The view looks good from here. I want to thank all those who have sacrificed so much so that the rest of us can live on safe ground. God bless my country. I'm proud to say I'm an American.

SAUCES AND GARNISHES

Caramel

In a heavy gauge pan, cook 1 cup sugar until it has turned to a shiny mahogany color. Immediately pour it into ½ c. hot water. Lower the heat and stir until the sugar is completely dissolved (2-3 minutes). Remove from heat. Let it cool. Pour into a glass jar. It can be kept at room temperature.

Attention: You have to keep your eyes constantly on the sugar during the cooking process. There is a very thin line between making caramel and making burnt sugar. If it tastes bitter, then you should practice with another batch.

Crispy Shallot/Aromatic Oil

This may be one stone, but you will get two birds here. The crispy shallot is indispensable as garnish for soup, salads, fried rice, noodles, sauces, etc. It has endless uses. Use the oil in marinades, salad dressings for things such as cole slaw, bean and green salads. Make a batch and let your imagination run crazy.

> 1 c. canola, corn or peanut oil
> ½ c. – ¾ c. thinly sliced shallots

In a heavy gauge medium-size pan (not aluminum), heat oil until hot but not smoking. Add shallots. Stir constantly until golden brown. Watch it like a hawk after 5 minutes. It's very important not to over cook. At the same time, it won't be crispy if it's under cooked. So, as soon as you see the color start to turn into a rich golden color, immediately remove the shallots with a slotted spoon. Drain on a paper towel. Cool completely before storing.

Store in a clean glass jar. To save space in the refrigerator, crispy shallots can be stored in a nice thick plastic bag that zips.

Crispy Garlic and Oil

In my catering kitchen, this oil is even more important than the shallot oil (which is saying something). I use it the same way as the shallot oil, but in different dishes.

> 2 c. corn, canola or peanut oil
> ¼ c. sesame oil
> 1 c. finely chopped garlic

Use a heavy gauge pan—not aluminum. Heat oil until hot (250 degrees F.). Add garlic and simmer until garlic turns golden. Turn heat off. Then remove garlic with a mesh spoon and spread it out on a paper towel to dry.

To the hot oil, add 4-5 whole dried hot peppers, plus 2 T. whole peppercorns. Let the chilies and peppercorns steep in the oil over night so that the oil's aroma is enriched. Pour the oil into a clean glass jar and store in the refrigerator.

Emergency Crispy Onion

There is the rare occasion when you run out of crispy shallots. This is a quicker version. It isn't as good, but it's better than nothing.

Heat ½ c. oil until hot, but not smoking. Remove from heat. Stir in 1/3 c. dried onion flakes. Let it cool in the oil, then strain and use as needed.

Scallion Oil

This oil is what Vietnamese culture, taste and style are all about. A dollop of this sauce makes any rice, noodles, or salad go from blah to something unique and special. Use it as a spread inside French bread with grilled beef and lemongrass. Now you're talking!

¼ c. canola or corn oil
½ c. chopped scallion

In a small, non-aluminum sauce pan, heat oil until hot, but not smoking. Add scallions. Swirl around 15-20 seconds. Remove from heat. The sauce is now ready to use. Leftovers can be refrigerated and kept for a few days.

Egg Crepe

Sprinkle some of this egg shredded thin on top of fried rice, noodles (Temple Salad), etc. It is a signature of Vietnamese cooking. It goes beyond garnish. It adds taste, texture and style to many dishes. A good non-stick skillet is essential. The rest is just good old fun.

In a small bowl mix:
2 eggs
½ tsp. fish or soy sauce
¼ tsp. black pepper
1 tsp. broth, soy milk or water

Heat skillet to medium high heat. Add a few drops of vegetable oil. Use a paper towel to spread the oil around to coat the skillet. Pour in enough egg to make a thin layer over the skillet. (Tilting the pan will help.) Take 15-20 seconds to cook. Turn over and cook the other side for 10 seconds. Repeat until all the egg mixture is used up. Stake and roll like a cylinder, then slice into thin strips. Refrigerate until ready to use. Never keep longer than three days.

Hot and Sour Daikon Carrot

This is a great touch to a green salad. A spoon or two in a bowl of fish sauce can be used for dressing or to top a sandwich. I always have a large jar of this item in my refrigerator.

In a large bowl:
　　3-4 c. daikon and carrots, cut into thin julienne slices

Dressing:
　　1 c. water
　　½ c. white vinegar
　　1 T. salt
　　3 T. sugar
　　2 serano, Thai Dragon, or birds eye chilies, sliced thin
　　2 T. (6 cloves) garlic, julienne cut

Mix well, then pack into a quart jar. This will keep for 3-4 weeks in the refrigerator.

Hot Mango Chutney

　　1 medium large ripe mango, cut into cubes (approximately 1 c.)
　　1 c. packed light brown sugar
　　2 c. water
　　½ c. golden raisins
　　½ c. rice or white vinegar
　　1 tsp. – 1 T. dried hot pepper flakes
　　½ c. crystallized ginger
　　2 tsp. salt

Put all ingredients in a medium-sized sauce pan. Bring to a boil. Lower heat. Cover. Simmer for 20 minutes. Use a hand blender and pulse a few times. Leave some chunks in the sauce, because that's a characteristic of chutney. This makes approximately 4 cups.

Tip: Use it as a dipping sauce for *hors d'oeuvres*, or as a glaze for an oven roast, or brush on meat on the grill.

Fresh Roasted Sesame

½ c. white sesame
1 T. black sesame

In a skillet over medium heat, pour in sesame seeds. Shake pan continuously for 2 to 3 minutes. As soon as the golden color emerges, remove from heat immediately. Pour sesame onto a cooled cookie sheet. Then, pour the seeds into a glass jar. Store in the refrigerator. Grind or use whole.

Tip: Before roasting sesame, it's helpful to put a shallow baking sheet in the freezer for five minutes. As soon as the seeds are golden, pour them onto the frozen sheet to cool. The result is a seed roasted to perfection. If the seeds are under roasted, they will have no taste. If they are over roasted, they will taste bitter.

Every-day Nuoc Cham

¾ c. water
½ c. white vinegar
½ c. sugar
2 T. to ¼ c. fresh crushed garlic
2-10 hot peppers, preferably Thai Bird Eye Chilies, or Thai Dragon, but, in a pinch, serano or jalapeno will do
¾ - 1 c. premium fish sauce

This makes approximately 3 cups. To say I love this sauce is an understatement. We go through jar after jar at my house. It is indispensable. Use soy sauce in place of fish sauce if you don't want anything to do with fish.

Hot Chili Oil

Why make hot oil instead of buying it ready made? Taste! (Saving money is the only good thing about buying the oil ready made.) There is no comparison between "store bought" and home made. For a superior quality, make it yourself. This is one item I always make sure I have in the refrigerator.

> ½ c. canola, corn or peanut oil
> 2 T. dark roasted sesame oil
> 1-2 T. crushed dried hot pepper

In a non-aluminum pan, combine the two oils. Bring almost to the smoking stage. Turn off the heat. Add pepper. When it's cooled, strain the chili off, and pour oil into a small glass jar. Refrigerate to keep it fresh. A few drops goes a long way.

Hot Chili Sauce

This is great for drizzling over dumplings, rice noodles or steamed vegetables. It has endless uses.

> ½ c. light soy sauce
> ¼ c. rice vinegar (or white)
> ¼ c. rice wine (mirin)
> 3 T. grated ginger
> 6 large cloves of garlic, minced
> 3 T. brown sugar
> 2 T. hot chili oil

This makes approximately 1 ½ c. Mix well. Store in a glass jar in the refrigerator.

Tahini Dressing

    1 c. water
    2 T. tahini paste
    ¼ c. soy sauce
    1/3 c. vinegar
    1-2 T. grated ginger
    ¼ c. brown sugar (or honey)
    ½ tsp. sesame oil
    ½ tsp. salt
    1/8 t. xathan gum (optional)*
    2 T. fresh roasted sesame seeds
    1 tsp. – 2 T. hot pepper flakes

*This is a natural thickening agent sold at health food stores.

This makes 2 cups.

Fish Sauce Dressing

For our specialty salads, such as grilled pork, grilled beef with lemongrass, spring rolls, fresh rolls, etc., this is a Vietnamese all purpose dressing. By the way, make sure to label all your jars as you put them into the refrigerator, or you'll be sorry.

    1 c. water
    ½ c. white vinegar
    ½ c. – 2/3 c. sugar*
    ½ c. fish sauce
    ¼ c. minced fresh garlic
    2-10 fresh hot chili peppers

*The amount of sugar depends on how salty the brand of fish sauce you are using is.

GLOSSARY

Here is my army of helpers and a brief description of how I use them:

Dry Ingredients:

Agar agar—This is a vegetable gel. It is seaweed, which has been boiled, pressed into a gel, then dried into flakes. The flakes will dissolve in hot liquid and thicken as they cool at room temperature.

Ascorbic—This is available at health food stores. It is also known as vitamin C. I use this when I need to add tartness to a dish, without adding aroma.

Textured soy protein—This is dried soy bean flakes. It is available at any health food store. It needs to be soaked before you can use it.

Dried shrimp—These are pungent and salty. They come in various sizes and prices. Soak before using and save liquid for sauce or broth.

Tapioca powder—This is made from cassava root. Depending on the dish, I use it to coat meat before stir frying because it provides a good "mouth feel."

Tapioca pearl—This is the same stuff, but in a little ball form, or granule. I use it mainly for desserts.

Water chestnut powder—This makes a fine coating for deep frying foods. It will not turn brown, so be careful not to overcook.

Five spice powder—As the name says, it's a mixture of cinnamon, star anise, fennel, cloves and ginger. Buy it in small quantities, because it gets stale quickly.

Dried shiitake mushrooms—These have a smoky flavor that fresh lacks.

Soak at least an hour prior to cooking time. Save the liquid for broth.

Black mushroom/tree ears/fungus—These are one and the same thing. They are also known as wood ears. Each will swell three to four times its original size. After soaking, wash and rinse well before use. Discard liquid.

Dried hot pepper—I buy this item whole, then grind them myself as needed for stir fry. For marinades and meat pastes, I use hot Mexican chilies.

Tamarind—This provides a pleasant tartness (lightly sweet) to soup or stir fry. Available dry in block or concentrated liquid. To save time, I recommend buying it in liquid form.

The Fresh:

Hot pepper—First choice for me would be Thai Dragon, but Bird Eyes Chilies are also good. In some cases, serano and jalapeno peppers are acceptable. Like a mail man, hot peppers never fail to deliver taste.

Egg plant—I prefer the long and slender ones. Where I live, I only find them in my garden around late August, and only when we have been blessed with warm weather.

Daikon—This is a large, white radish. It is pungent with a hint of pepper. Use it in soup, stew, stir fry, salad, etc.

Cabbage—I use it in soup and stir fry. Stuff with tofu or meat.

Jicama—This is a tuber with a brownish skin. It has a cool, crisp and lightly sweet taste. It stays firm after cooking.

Ginger root—It is important to use fresh ginger. Dried ginger is unacceptable. If you have extra, freeze it for later use.

Kaffir lime leaves—These are available in specialty food stores, most likely in frozen form. Aromatic in soup, stew, curry and Thai style cuisine.

Lemongrass—There is no substitute for this item. Use it in fresh or frozen form. Dried lemongrass is awful.

The Bottles:

Wine—A good bottle of rice wine is essential. A good rule of thumb is to taste it before using. Let's face it, if the ingredient doesn't taste good by itself, how is it going to help your dish?

Mirin—This is Japanese seasoning wine with a pleasant aroma and is lightly sweet. It's my personal favorite for many dishes.

Soy sauce—A good bottle of soy sauce is just as important as a bottle of wine, because there is a layer of chemistry between the two ingredients. My every day soy sauce is superior light soy sauce from Pearl River Bridge. Dark soy and mushroom soy is good to add color.

Golden Mountain Sauce—This is a Thai seasoning sauce. I use this to create a different dimension to certain dishes.

Fish sauce—This is made from fermented fish. It is the back bone in Vietnamese, Philipine, Thai and Cambodian cooking. There are no substitutes for this item if you want to make it authentic. In some recipes, I compromise only if I have to. Don't be scared off by its aroma. Fish sauce will mellow after cooking. I recommend buying the premium grade for better taste.

Oyster sauce—This is made from oyster extract. Purchase the premium grade and stay away from the cheap ones. A good oyster sauce will add depth and flavor.

Vinegar—Not all vinegars are created equal. If you don't have rice vinegar handy, use the all purpose white vinegar. Rice vinegar, however, has a pleasant grain-like taste. White vinegar is harsh in comparison. For salad dressing, experiment with flavored vinegars.

Sesame oil—Go for the dark roasted sesame oil that is made in Japan, Kadoya brand. The pale one has no taste or aroma. Taste it before using. If it tastes stale and rancid, it's time to get another bottle. Remember, this is a seasoning oil. It is not for cooking. A little goes a long way.

Chili garlic sauce from Lee Kum Kee—This is good for adding a little kick to stir fry. It's available in specialty food sections at most grocery stores.

Sriracha chili sauce—We use this sauce in our house the way other people use ketchup. Hot, spicey, with a pleasant kick of sweetness.

Chili garlic sauce from Huy Fong Foods—This is a Vietnamese brand of chili sauce. Hot, without sugar. Add a little to your soup, only if you can handle it.

Hoisin sauce—Last but not least. This is a pleasant, sweet and salty brown bean sauce. I can't imagine eating a bowl of beef and noodle soup without this sauce mixed with sriracha chili. It's a marriage made in heaven.

Noodles:

After rice, noodles are my favorite. Everybody can cook noodles, but to prepare a dish of noodles to perfection, one needs practice. Don't hesitate to experiment. Try as many different kinds as you can.

Flat rice noodles are the most commonly used in Vietnamese cuisine. We use these for soup and stir fry. For salads and soups, we use rice sticks (also known as *bun*). There is the extra thin rice noodle, known as *Banh hoi*. The Chinese egg noodle is also popular. The noodle section at an Asian market can be intimidating and confusing for the beginner. Here is a quick run down that will, I hope, shed some light on that section.

Cellophane Noodles: These are made from the starch of mung beans. They are also known as bean thread. These need to be soaked for at least ½ hour prior to cooking time. Use for stir fry, soup, salad, binding agent for meat (such as our stuffed tomatoes). These come in many different sizes. My favorite is the small 8 pack or 8 oz. blocks.

Rice Noodles: In Vietnamese, these are called *Banh pho*. (They are flat.) The wide version of these is good for stir fry. The medium one is good for soup. And the smaller version is good for Pad Thai. You may cook any rice noodle straight from their dried stage. Simply plunge them in boiling water. However, they are much better if you soak them ahead of time. Soaking cuts the cooking time in half and you will have better results.

Rice Sticks: In Vietnamese, these are called bun. (They are round.) Cook directly from dried state. This takes about 5 minutes. Drain and rinse with cold water before using. If you soak these ahead of time, cooking will only take 2-3 minutes. These are good in salad, soups, salad rolls, etc.

Extra Thin Rice Noodles: These delicate little strands team up with roasted pork or roasted duck. Soak first, drain, then plunge into boiling water. Stir them constantly and watch them like a hawk. Cooking only takes 1-2 minutes, depending on the manufacturer. Rinse well with cold water and toss with Scallion Oil before serving.

Chinese Egg Noodles: These are yellow, dried or fresh. They are good for stir fry or tossed with Toasted Sesame and Chili Sauce for a quick and tasty side dish.

Chinese Wheat Flour Noodles: These are made from wheat flour and water. They are available at most Asian markets in dried form, round or flat. They can be used in stir fry or for hearty soups. Cook with caution. They easily stick together and the directions on the package are, most of the time, way off base.

Tapioca Noodles: These are translucent noodles with a chewy texture. They are one of my favorite noodles. I always soak them first, then blanch in boiling water for 2-3 minutes. Rinse very well in cold water and drain thoroughly. Then they are ready for soup or stir fry.

Soba: These are a Japanese buck wheat noodles. I love the nutty taste of these noodles as much as I love the nutritious value they provide. Delicious hot or cold. Try some with grilled chicken and Tahini Dressing for a memorable chicken salad.

Somen: These are another popular Japanese noodle. You will most likely notice these noodles on the shelf because they are neatly packaged with a pretty ribbon. These are good in either hot or cold dishes.

Udon: These are extra thick and fat white round noodles. These are wheat noodles in the States, but in Vietnam they are made with rice as well. I use this noodle for soup and in certain kinds of salads.

CPSIA information can be obtained
at www.ICGtesting.com
Printed in the USA
BVHW041300061120
592720BV00013B/212

9 781412 068895